I'm Not With The Band

I'm Not With The Band

Finding Your Own Rhythm for Success

Tony Capullo

iUniverse, Inc.
New York   Bloomington

I'm Not With The Band
Finding Your Own Rhythm for Success

iUniverse books may be ordered through booksellers or by contacting:

iUniverse
1663 Liberty Drive
Bloomington, IN 47403
www.iuniverse.com
1-800-Authors (1-800-288-4677)

ISBN: 978-1-4401-2964-3 (pbk)
ISBN: 978-1-4401-2965-0 (ebk)

Printed in the United States of America

iUniverse rev. date: 3/25/2009

DEDICATION

This book is dedicated to Robert Capullo—I'm still hustling, Dad—and to my daughter, Kaitlin Marie, who is the most precious person to me on Earth. I love you.

Acknowledgments

It is at times difficult to express the gratitude I have for the people in my life who accompany me in my incredible journey, but this is for them: David Herdlinger, who has influenced me so profoundly throughout my career. This book would not have been possible without you, that's for sure; Susana Walls, for the countless hours extracting information and who has now brought us here—this is as much your book as it is mine; to Janice Drescher and Jeff Burrows for teaching me the significance of alignment, clarity, and focus—you can bet that I will forever be working *on* the business and not *in* it. To Gerald Dunham and Dean Sadler, I can't find the words to express what you have meant to my career and to my life. Thank you for allowing me to live my dream. This journey would not have been half as much fun without you. To my mother, Nancy, who told me when I was young, "You get out of something what you put into it." I never forgot those words and I will never forget the undying support that I received throughout my life. If some of my personal stories in this book are not familiar to you, we can discuss them at dinner. To Meghan, the bartender, wherever you are: If I ever make the band, I'll mail you a backstage pass.

Foreword

From the moment I met Tony Capullo, he has been all about "yes." I've been coaching business owners to build a business that serves their deepest wishes in life for over 20 years. Even though what it takes to build a successful business is the same each time, every business owner is different and all bring uniqueness to the endeavor of creating more of what they want in their lives. There were two things that stood out about Tony from the very start that caught my attention. The first is that he has a very strong sense of who he is and isn't about to modify that to fit any particular mold. The second is that he has a burning desire to learn everything he can get his hands on to close the gap between where he is and where he wants to be in his life. The result has been a growing momentum, fueled by inspiration and focus that is producing extraordinary results in his business and his life because of his leadership. He turns frustrations and obstacles into opportunities by allowing them to lead him to more of what he wants.

Pinpointed focus brings with it opportunities. This is the arena of inspiration that invites others to join simply because it feels good to be around such clarity and self-alignment. Holding the ground of one's well-being front and center is a tool for navigating through the ups and downs of life that keeps you on a steady course to your dreams. Tony Capullo is an inspiration for those who choose to travel down that sacred road.

Janice Drescher
Master Success Code Coach

INTRODUCTION

A few years ago, I was on a short business trip up to the Northeast. I landed at the airport, collected my luggage and cabbed it to the hotel. After checking in, I threw on a pair of jeans, a ball cap, my favorite worn-out boots and a casual shirt, and headed down to the hotel bar.

The place was packed with yuppies and "suits" rubbing elbows and talking business. I looked around and realized that I was the only one not wearing business clothes. Remember that old *Sesame Street* song, "One of these things is not like the others; one of these things just doesn't belong?" Well, that described me at that moment.

As I sat there by myself, chilling out, the girl behind the bar, Meghan, came over and started to make small talk. After a few minutes, she looked at me and asked, "So, are you with the band?"

"No, I'm not with the band," I responded, amused. "I can't sing worth a damn." She obviously had sized me up and, between the ripped jeans, tattoos and earrings, figuring that I was a renegade from an MTV video.

That wasn't the first or the last time someone has asked me a question like that; one based on an assumption that was formed according to my appearance. The words and situations vary, but the perceptions are the same. I simply don't fit the stereotypical businessman mold.

I know a lot of talented, creative people who are involved in business or want to be. But they're smothering their creativity and talents and sabotaging their success because they're trying to fit the image of what they think a businessperson should look and act like.

I firmly believe that you can only be successful when you are true to yourself. Your unique abilities and your passion are the most valuable assets you have to offer. But the world won't see them, benefit from them, or reward you for them if you're preoccupied with "fitting in."

A friend once told me about a very successful Atlanta attorney who has a ponytail that hangs past his waist. Despite breaking the stereotype for a lawyer, he has a flourishing law practice. Kudos to that guy!

In the first part of the book I share of bit of my history. My intention is not to portray myself as a guru. I've made plenty of mistakes. I don't have all the answers and I don't pretend to hold myself up as a role model (God forbid). But I have been very successful at being myself, and that has made me successful in business.

The second part of this book is meant to be a practical resource of wisdom gleaned from many knowledgeable and experienced sources that provide tools and insights for being successful in a job or business. Most of these "bits of wisdom" aren't earthshaking, they're just practical tips that I've learned over the years. And they've been proven to work.

I hope what I share with you will encourage you to follow a path to discover your own rhythm, even in the face of criticism. I hope it will inspire you to step out of your comfort zone, overcome fear, risk failure and take a shot at trying to accomplish new things in life.

As motivational guru Tony Robbins says, "Success leaves clues." That's why I study successful people. I like to pick their brains and learn from them. I figure that if someone else does something and it works, it will probably work for me, too. I compare it to a cookbook recipe. If you follow the steps and use the same ingredients, you will get a similar result.

So, if you feel as if you're pressed up against a ceiling, I hope this book expands your horizons. If you're holding back because of fear, I hope this book challenges you to reach for higher goals. If you wish you had more enthusiasm, I hope this book sparks your passion. And, if you want more success, I hope this book inspires you to pursue your unique vision with all the energy you possess, until you achieve results beyond your wildest dreams.

Tony Capullo
Somewhere in Fort Lauderdale
November 2007

CHAPTER 1: HUSTLE

My father often told me, "Approach everything the way Pete Rose plays baseball. Always hustle." He also told me that even if I were to strike out to *run* back to the dugout. I must have been eight years old at the time he gave this advice, and I know that no eight-year-old wants to run back to the dugout after striking out or making an error. But to "hustle?"

I guess I understand why he would use that term; after all, my father knew all about hustle. I'm not talking about knowing how to run a shell game, but about the kind of hustling that involves hard work and immediate action. I remember when my sister and I were small, my father held two jobs at once, stocking vending machines and helping out in a bowling alley. All the while he did his best to raise a family. While he didn't have the benefit of a college education to help him get ahead in life, he had early mornings and late nights to get him through what needed to be done.

Just as he had the ability to work hard, he also had a laid-back demeanor to get him through the day. My father hardly ever angered, rarely cussed and never drank or smoked. His mood was always upbeat and his sense of humor was dry but lovable. While he also rarely dispensed advice, the one thing he *did* drill into my head at an early age was the importance of "hustling," always motivating me to get moving and take action—and that meant even running back to the dugout.

Hard work is not a foreign concept in my family. My maternal grandfather, Nick DeLavic, also helped to instill in me the importance of a strong work ethic. Never having graduated from high school, he owned and operated a successful business building nursing homes and shopping centers. As a five-year-old, I recall admiring him. Every morning on his way to work he would stop by our house, dressed in his suit and carrying his briefcase. It was then, based on my grandfather's commanding presence, that I decided I was going to become a businessman. Oh yes, I wanted the whole thing: suit and tie, briefcase and to smell like Old Spice. (Little did I know that years later I would despise wearing business suits and, needless to say, I passed on the Old Spice.)

A Sandwich, a Banana and Two Pencils, Please

My plan to become a businessman started early. In kindergarten, my Superman lunchbox became my briefcase. I proudly carried it each morning to my "job." To make it official, I asked my mother to place two pencils in the lunchbox, just in case I had a busy day.   When my grandfather passed away in 1973, the image of a businessman was firmly etched in my mind.

In August 1977, right before my thirteenth birthday, our family moved from upstate New York to Fort Lauderdale, Florida. My father, seeking self-employment and greener pastures, went into a partnership with a friend operating a Carvel ice cream store.   Unfortunately, it was a short-lived enterprise, since he and his partner operated using very different moral compasses (I'm being diplomatic here).

As a result, the stress of my dad's struggles to earn money disrupted our family life.   In order to mind the store, he was not home as often as he wanted to be, and the stress of being in a partnership with someone he couldn't trust wore on him. My father was honest to a fault, so it was difficult for him to understand how anyone would not embrace and live by his business ethic. Those years were difficult, but they allowed me to see the example my father had set being an upright individual, respectful of the law and devoted to his family.

After high school, I studied accounting at the University of Florida in Gainesville. At the time, UF's accounting school was ranked the second best in the country. It almost seems like a miracle that I graduated, considering how much of my study time was spent with my buddy, Alan Saltman, listening to the same songs on the jukebox and downing one-dollar drinks at the now defunct Purple Porpoise, a local dive. While my initial plan had been to attend the University of Miami, the sight of UF's majestic brick buildings, overwhelming sense of school spirit, the opportunity to live away from home, and the gorgeous female coeds motivated me to make the choice to become a Gator.

It was during my sophomore year that I learned a real "life-based" accounting practice. It started with my receipt of a Citibank credit card with a whopping $300 credit limit. Being a poor college student suddenly presented with a $300 spending pass, I felt like I had received an early Christmas present. I quickly calculated that $300 could buy a lot of beers and dates, and before the Citibank envelope hit the ground, I was out ordering rounds of drinks. It also didn't take long to see how far $300 could go.

One Saturday afternoon, our backpacks filled with beer and ice, Alan and I drove from Gainesville and spent the day floating on inner tubes down the Itchitucknee River, contemplating our college lives. On the way home, sunburned and buzzed, we made a pit stop for gas. After filling the tank, I went inside to pay with the credit card. To my surprise the station attendant simply confiscated it: no questions asked, no courtesy inquiry as to whether I had another card, just a flat out confiscation. Turns out I had exceeded my limit.

As four people waited in line behind me, I watched the attendant pull a pair of scissors and cut my card. With no cash on hand, and now a full tank, Alan proceeded to write a check. The attendant stopped him and said, "Son, I don't take personal checks." Alan and I looked at each other blankly, after which Alan replied, "Well, Mister, you'd better get a hose and start siphoning the gas out of my tank, because we have no other way to pay you."

The attendant took the check.

My college years were a mixture of adventures, music, a few classes to break up the monotony and a few beers here and there. I am not sure where my Superman lunchbox/businessman dream went during this time, but it was not at the forefront of my mind. I think I managed to get through by my desire to make my parents proud and the understanding that it was the necessary (and expected) thing for me to do.

Lots of Debits and Very Little Credit

In December of 1986, after graduation, I landed my first real job. It was at Coopers & Lybrand out of Fort Myers, Florida, one of the largest and most prestigious accounting firms in the nation during this time. Most new grads would have felt like a big shot to have landed that job, but it didn't take long before I felt more like an indentured servant. Dressed in my once coveted business suit and starched white shirt "uniform," I'd hunch over my ten-key adding machine in my second-floor cubicle. The hours were long and the work was boring as hell.

When we worked overtime, which was often, we banked "points" that could be exchanged for time off from work. My coworkers bragged about how many points they had "banked" and how they were planning to spend their time off. But that made no sense to me. I came to work to earn money and get promoted, not to earn points to get away from work.

My defining moment with my Coopers & Lybrand career came one day as I was eating lunch in the office break room and reading the sports section of the newspaper. Pete Rose had just been banned from baseball for allegedly betting on the sport. Here was arguably the greatest hitter in the history of the game, being slapped with a lifetime ban. Having grown up a Rose fan, I was stunned and disappointed. My co-workers, on the other hand, showed no interest in discussing this development. Instead, they continued their conversation about the financial auditing standards for inventorying meat in the freezer of a country club client.

I took a few moments to gather my thoughts on the situation. In my opinion, one of the best players in the history of baseball had just been kicked out of the game; my childhood idol. Meanwhile, I was sitting in a room with people who actually were enthusiastically brainstorming on how to count slabs of meat.

I needed to get a new job.

Thinking that everything would be fine if I changed employers, I accepted an offer from a smaller CPA firm. Unfortunately, that job was even worse. It, too, was all about billable hours, debits, credits and inventory. There was intense pressure to put dollars in the firm's pocket, while I wanted dollars in *my* pocket.

On the outside, I was the go-getter—the first one at the office in the morning and the last one to leave at night—but on the inside I was miserable. Everyone else loved the environment, which included spending tax season sorting through garbage bags and shoeboxes of our clients' receipts and tax documents. I hated every minute of it. I didn't care to know how much John Smith was spending a year on meals and travel; John Smith was living it up while I rummaged through his receipts. If anything, I was motivated to seek greener pastures and my own freedom. After enduring twelve months that seemed like twelve years, I resigned.

Although my parents did their best to be understanding, they were deeply disappointed in my decision to throw in the towel on my accounting career. They had taken great pride in telling people that their son was an accountant. The problem was that their son was an accounting misfit. "Just get a job with a salary, with some security," my father advised. I could understand his point of view; his job security put food on the table for our family. He wanted me to be able to provide for mine when the time came. I, however, didn't feel that accounting was the way for me to find security. It didn't provide satisfaction with my job, or, for that matter, happiness. I knew there was something bigger and better out there for me, and I was determined to find it.

Gaining Clarity

As disgruntled as I was working in the smaller firm, I was also beginning to get a clearer picture of where I wanted to go and what I wanted to be. My experience had taught me that I definitely didn't want to sit in a cubicle poring over receipts and discussing beef inventory.

I started making a list of my goals. At the top of my list was "to be successful in business so that I can live comfortably and retire on my own terms." I wanted to be my own boss and call the shots. (I've never enjoyed taking orders.) I also found I didn't like busting my back for a fixed salary. I didn't like hoping for a Christmas bonus only to receive instead a holiday card with a $25 Wal-Mart gift certificate inside. I wanted to accumulate wealth and surround myself with smart people—people of *my* choosing, whom I genuinely liked (who knew who Pete Rose was); people I could learn from.

It was obvious that the only way for me to achieve all of this was to become my own boss. But making that leap was a scary thought. I had no cash reserves to start a business, let alone to pay expenses while I launched it. I also had no idea as to what business I would go into or what service I would offer. The odds were stacked against me, but I was determined that I would find my passion and convert it into a long-term moneymaking venture.

One day, as I stood in the checkout line at the supermarket, I observed a number of older gentlemen employees bagging items and pushing carts to the customers' cars. "That will *never* be me," I resolved. I wanted the ability to retire on my terms. I didn't want to be in my sixties, having to bag groceries to get by. No way.

Fear can be paralyzing or it can be used to drive you forward. That day, the fear of failure drove me toward success. Watching those poor guys push those carts made me even more determined to create my own destiny. I am a believer that you can have just about anything you want in life if you want it badly enough. There is always a way if you are committed.

A friend once asked me what it took to maintain my health and physical fitness. At that time I was waking up at 2:30 in the morning and working out by 3:30, so I explained to them my regimen and my diet. I assured her she could do the same thing.

"No," she answered, "I could never do that."

"It depends on how much you want it," I replied.

Since then, that statement has become one of my favorite mottos: "It depends on how much you want it." That says it all.

Running Toward the Sun

After leaving the second CPA firm, I felt a strong need to get away. Having always loved the ocean, I took what money I had—about $2,000—and bought a plane ticket for St. Thomas, U.S Virgin Islands. I did some minor planning before my departure: In case there wasn't enough money left for me to make my car payments when I returned,

I decided to park my car three blocks from my apartment and chose to cover it up with the hopes that it wouldn't be found and repossessed. I figured that, worst-case scenario, the bank would take my car and I would ride the bus with a great tan.

With my car "secured" and money in my pocket, I boarded the plane.

It was my second night on the island when I met a guy named Curtis White. I found out that Curtis was a controller for a company that delivered overnight mail back to the States. He was soft-spoken, laid back and, as I recall, a pretty impressive beer drinker. Over drinks I told Curtis that I had a degree in accounting and that I was running from a bad start to what I thought would be a great career.

Once he heard the words "accounting degree," he begged me to help him process some inventory for the company that he was working for.

"I just quit working and I'm here on vacation," I told him.

Curtis was desperate. After he pleaded long enough (and offered an irresistible arrangement—he would pay for my hotel room during my stay), I finally relented. It had only been three days since I had left the CPA firm, and here I was working again. But this locale was a far cry from the drab cubicle overrun with receipts and frozen beef inventory adventures.

Curtis and I quickly became friends, and I helped him a few more times while I was there. The work was actually enjoyable. I would show up at the airplane hangar (the company's headquarters) in shorts, flip-flops and a tank top. It sure beat the hell out of a suit and tie.

My excursion to St Thomas, while probably not the smartest thing to do at the time, was a total blast. Not only did I earn a free hotel stay, skinny dip with two girls who celebrated passing their bar exam, learn to drive on the left side of the road, sun myself and drink boat drinks on Megan's Bay, but I also broke the monotony of my career. I felt I definitely earned plenty of "banked points" for my efforts.

Looking back, I don't know whether to laugh or be horrified. Obviously, I'm a different person today. (No, really, I am). It's amazing that my parents didn't disown me. While I'm not proud of many things I did during this time, in hindsight the experiences were necessary to help me learn and understand what my true desires and objectives were and how to go about realizing them.

One thing is important: In the midst of my St. Thomas adventure, I found I did the right thing: I followed my instincts. My parents and the "responsible" voice in my head were telling me to get a job, any job. That was the safe, respectable thing to do. But my gut was telling me that I needed a change of scenery to get my bearings.

I listened to my gut. It was right. It usually is.

When you're successful, people tend to think you've always been that way. But I've come to realize that many, if not all, successful people endure some down times before they make it. I'd always known I had what it took to be successful, but it took time to find the right place.

Bad experiences are often blessings in disguise. They leave such strong impressions on you that you'll do whatever it takes to avoid repeating them. My accounting experiences motivated me to make a change.

CHAPTER 2: BE PREPARED...BE VERY PREPARED

Everyone's heard the expression, "When opportunity knocks, open the door." While most of us wait for opportunity to come knocking, it should be understood that there are times when you must take the initiative and find a door to kick down.

Finding myself with a clearer head after returning from my St. Thomas hiatus, I was determined to find something I would love doing for the rest of my life. Having never been intimidated by size, I knocked on the door of the biggest hospital in Fort Myers, Southwest Florida Regional Medical Center.

The prospect of working in a healthcare facility brought both excitement and deep-rooted childhood memories to mind. My father was once the Director of Social Services at Silver Haven Nursing Home in Schenectady, New York, the same facility my grandfather had helped to build in 1968. During my father's employment at Silver Haven, I often visited him and observed his pleasant interaction with both the patients and his staff. It was this recollection, the idea of working with an array of people in contrast to the group of stuffy accountants that I had escaped from weeks before, that lured and motivated me to apply for a position at the Medical Center. I saw the possibility of doing and being more than a numbers cruncher.

"There's only one job opening in the accounting department," Brian Regan, the Accounting Department's Controller, advised me upon my inquiry about any open positions. "It's for a Data Manager, and you're overqualified."

"Besides," he continued, "you don't have hospital experience, and someone with experience has applied for the job."

He tried his best to dissuade me. But in my mind, I didn't even know what a Data Manager did. Truth be told, I also really didn't care. I needed a job. I needed *that* job.

"Just give me a 30-day trial." I proposed. "If I don't impress the hell out of you in 30 days, I'll leave."

The fact that I was running out of money made me more determined than ever to get my foot in the door.

It would be nice if I could say that Brian hired me that day, but he didn't. Instead, he said he'd think about it. I helped him think about it by calling him every other day. My phone having been disconnected, I called him mostly from pay phones on a makeshift "call and remind" schedule.

I was determined to get the job. I needed it. There was no Plan B.

By my tenth call, Brian gave in. As soon as I heard him say, "Come on in; you're hired," I felt immediate relief. The thoughts of paid bills, freedom from my telephone booth offices and the personal satisfaction of being employed allowed me to breathe again.

To this day, I consider that job to be the turning point of my career. My 30-day trial was a success and had me flying high. In no time, I grasped the duties of a Data Manager and had professionally gained more than I had ever expected. I had pursued and seized an opportunity, and with it, an atmosphere that was better than I had imagined: terrific people, rewarding work and decent cafeteria food. Utopia!

After several weeks as a Data Manager, the departure of an immediate supervisor led to the assignment of additional duties. Opportunity was now knocking on my self-built door and I was more than happy to accept whatever it brought. As my scope of responsibilities expanded and the job became more challenging, I stepped up to the professional possibilities. I followed well-intended advice seeing it as an opportunity to grow and develop. One piece of advice came from a friend who worked in the regional office. He informed me that in order to know how the hospital ran, I should offer to prepare the operating budget. He made sure to inform me that the process was a grueling one, but he also assured me that I would come to learn the place inside and out. That was all I needed: A challenge to learn something in its entirety. And why not? I already knew what grueling was—I had been an accountant for three and a half years.

With a new focus in mind, I asked to be put in charge of the hospital's operating budget. My responsibilities tripled. The task was arduous and demanding. I worked long hours, participated in never-ending meetings and became well acquainted with the incessant griping of various department heads regarding what to include in their budgets. In the end, I remained committed and enjoyed the process.

I found my hard work and dedication paying off as management rewarded me with various tokens of appreciation. During my first year and for three months running I was the recipient of the "Employee of the Month" award along with a hard-earned 6 percent pay raise (the maximum raise allowed per year). And while Human Resources attempted to halt the creation of positions based on supposed "special treatment," hospital administration overruled the opposition and created that which was necessary to compensate for my hard work. I was seeing my rewards compounding on a regular basis. I kept myself motivated by the results.

By my second year with Southwest Regional, I had received a cumulative pay increase of 72.5 percent and, out of a handful of employees I received the "Excellent Performer Award," which included a $1,000 bonus along with an invitation to the annual awards banquet. However, before I could write my acceptance speech (I still laugh at the concept of me writing an "acceptance speech"), Human Resources objected and noted that I now held a managerial position and was therefore ineligible. As a result, I passed the award on to a co-worker in my department.

It was also during this second year that Columbia / HCA bought Southwest Regional from Basic American Medical, Inc. As with most acquisitions, the new owners' first matter of business was to replace the CEO and CFO in order to install their own management team. Shortly after the changing of the guards came the layoffs. After the layoffs began the necessary cost-cutting measures, such as the elimination of overtime. It was a miserable period, and I figured it was only a matter of time before I, too, got the ax. Employees were leaving in droves, and not always voluntarily. Those of us who remained seemed to be walking on eggshells. Every day felt like it could be my day.

And then, late one afternoon, the summons came: Jay Jarrell, the interim CFO, asked to see me. I was almost hyperventilating as I walked down the hall to his office. It felt like a walk to the execution chamber. I reviewed my parting thoughts: "I've done a great job here, and now I am getting canned." I even thought, albeit fleetingly, that maybe I should have extended my stay in St. Thomas.

As I sat in the chair across from Jay's desk, my hands were shaking. We made some brief small talk before he finally got to the punch.

"Tony…" he began. Time seemed to stand still as he spoke.

"We've identified you as a superstar," he continued, "and we want you to stick around." Pause. "And to show you your value, we are giving you an additional $10,000 per year raise."

My emotions had gone from blinding fear to complete confusion. I don't think I knew my name at that moment. It was all very surreal, but I had to respond. Upon gathering my faculties, I replied, "This is great Jay, but I need one more thing." Hey, I was feeling lucky, and why not push it when the ax is no longer over your neck? I went ahead with my requests. "I need to know that the people in my department have job security and that you won't cut their hours or their overtime." I felt this was the least I could do for the hard work and loyalty of my team. It was by way of their participation that the tasks were always completed on time, in detail, and with supporting facts. I couldn't do the work without them, and having fostered their support and involvement had paid off in my success. I could only return the acknowledgment by asking for job security on their behalf.

In the end, Jay agreed to my requests and I struggled to not leave his office doing a jig.   After all, I had entered with a grim vision of what was going to happen and instead I had emerged victorious based on my hard work and passion. I learned that when you have passion for something, in spite of all the work, the pressures, the unreasonable demands, the work itself does not matter. Instead of focusing on the pressure, I focused on the bottom line. The bottom line was now paying off for me, and in turn for those who shared the same dedication and viewpoint.

It doesn't take long for such news—positive or negative—to travel, and the realization that my requests were granted drew the attention of many. While for some this was cause for celebration, a number of hospital managers became deeply upset upon learning that a non-revenue producing department did not have to terminate employees or cut overtime.

In a hospital environment, with the pressures of providing adequate patient support staff and yet facing necessary budget cuts, the granting of my request baffled many of my fellow staff. However, in my mind, those that complained had no true grounds for complaints. That they had failed to obtain special considerations because they didn't ask for any was not an excuse to grieve. Plain and simple, what you don't ask for, you usually don't get.

By 1992, we were a flagship hospital in a five-hospital region and I was now reporting directly to the CFO. For budgeting purposes, the corporate office gave each hospital a net income target and the hospital had to make it work. It was like putting together a very complicated puzzle, and it created a pressure-cooker of an atmosphere. Everything had to fit perfectly and, in the end, result in a seamless picture.

The grumbling was rampant and I discovered that I had an ability to work well under pressure. My position had provided me with an opportunity to learn how to address the continuous last-minute corporate requests that were often due in less than 24 hours. I found that the only way I could deliver on such demands was to always be prepared. Being prepared meant current and accurate data at your immediate disposal. A flagship hospital lives and breathes by this information. It was imperative to have the right data, the correct numbers, accurate maximized reimbursement figures, and to ensure that all billing and collection reporting data was accurate. There was no way around these demands. You either had them or you spent the night sweating over how to get them and compile the report. It was part of the job. Crumbling under pressure was not an option, and delivering was mandatory.

I directed my team by simply stating the truth: "Be one step ahead of me. I'll be one step ahead of them. Always think they are going to ask for something. And when you do something—*anything*—make sure you know the reason you did it. Be prepared. Be *very* prepared."

While several Budget Directors had difficulties advising Department Managers that they were unable to obtain what the managers were requesting, I had no problem giving my budget directives in order to stay on target. It was much easier for me to hear and accept the gripes from a department head at my facility regarding the strict adherence to budget cuts. It was not so easy to hear and accept the complaints from a corporate CFO about not staying within the given guidelines. To corporate, the figures they provided for us to adhere to were not merely "suggested"; they were set in stone, and their stance was, "You have X amount to work with, now make it fit. Oh, and as a side note, just in case you're wondering, make sure it makes sense."

It was then my job to ensure that we adhered to the demands. Adherence meant reduced corporate complaints. Reduced complaints meant less sweating and less pressure. In the end, even those who griped benefited.

Aside from having the correct data, it was necessary to present the data in a manner that was logical and informative. It was a puzzle without a reference image. All I knew was that the pieces had to fit and I had to compose that image. This required time. I had to analyze the numbers, understand what was being put together and know where to make the necessary adjustments. Where most people didn't want to stay at work past six or seven o'clock, I worked late into the night to get the job done. Working until 3 a.m. was not uncommon for me.

On one particular evening (one of many), I needed to refuel. The hospital cafeteria had already closed and, with my stomach now eating at my spine, I found my way to the Physicians' Lounge. For the record, the Physicians' Lounge is as mysterious a location for the non-physician as the Teachers' Lounge was to most of us back in school, a members-only type of club. At 3 a.m., I just wanted food and I didn't really care who was allowed in or not. I soon discovered that this lounge was a Mecca of goodness—fresh-cut fruit, cold cuts, juices, and bottled water; a feast fit for a king. In my ravenous state, I was pleased to have stumbled upon such a bounty. As I stuffed my face with grapes (picture the old Chip and Dale chipmunks for this next part), I was joined in the lounge by a cleaning lady who had come to perform her nightly task. After taking in my attire and, no doubt, my actions, she asked suspiciously, "Are you a doctor?" With my cheeks bulging and my hands poised to grab the next item, the only response I could give was, "Uh…" It wasn't a question or an answer; it was the only sound the grapes allowed me to make. I laugh now at the recollection of that night and how I didn't question or wonder what I needed to do to get the job done. I just did it.

On one occasion, I worked for six months with the budget directors from four other facilities to respond to a corporate request. Aside from obtaining the necessary data, we were asked to present the material. During this time, no one cared who took the lead or who did what. Our primary focus was to make it work. We weren't out for glory, but instead we were thankful for any help that came. Working as a team, we backed our findings in order to present consistent and true data to the corporate offices. As before, we backed our information with reasons as to why. Nothing was done without an explanation.

Our presentation day for the corporate hot shots finally arrived. In a small room, before a stone-faced audience, we were asked to present our findings, one by one. The demands were simple: stand up, present, show the type of progress your facility was making on the budget and pull a rabbit out of your hat while you were at it. Sure, easy as pie. If you this was not your first rodeo and you were a master rider.

The first presenter is always the sacrificial lamb, and today was no exception. The corporate representative barely allowed him a full minute to speak before he started waving his hands, shaking his head in disgust and shouting, "No! No! No!" Silence ensued.

"This is not what we want. Get your ass outta here and go fix it!"

I learned that formalities are quickly done away with once you get behind conference room doors. Panicked, I wondered if could sneak out a window without anyone noticing. Maybe if I left my papers in a neat pile with a note they wouldn't even care if I went missing.

I watched the limping lamb slink out of the room. He had set the stage for the rest of us, but we could only go up from here. I had been thorough in my preparation to specifically avoid the very humiliation my teammate had experienced. I worked diligently to cover all areas that were requested and made sure to understand what I was expected to convey. And yet I trembled at the importance of this presentation and my determination to shine. But I had worked hard and, in the end, as I knew it would, that hard work paid off.

After the success of my presentation, I was asked to assist other hospitals with preparing their budgets. Compared to what I'd had to do at my location, these other facilities were easy. Opportunity was definitely pounding on my door. I made sure to greet it with a celebratory drink.

By the fall of 1992, I had been directly involved and had assisted with the preparation of budgets for the other four Southwest Region Columbia hospitals while also having maintained the duties and responsibilities of my full-time position. I was considerably younger than the budget directors I was assisting, but they harbored no resentment towards me for it, or the fact that I was instructed to guide them. I was only 28 years old and had been in the field and position a smidgeon of time in comparison to their years of education and expertise.

As my career advanced, I met my first professional role model. Chuck Hall had become the new CEO of Southwest Regional, and his work ethic was beyond impressive. Filled with high energy, dedication and a sense of purpose, Chuck was like no other CEO I had encountered thus far. In many cases, CEOs are mere figureheads. In my time with the hospital I rarely witnessed those in the noted position interacting or truly accessible. But Chuck was different. Traversing the hallways at 6:30 am, noting the minute details of the facility was evident proof of a hands-on leader. I had heard that prior to his move to Southwest Regional Chuck had won a high recognition award for best CEO within the organization. After observing his methods, it was no surprise to me why.

Every morning, by the time I was pulling into the hospital parking lot, Chuck was already in action. One Sunday, as I was working on the hospital budget, I heard loud pounding on the main door to the Accounting Department. Surprised that anyone in the building would need accounting assistance that day, I opened it. To my great surprise, Chuck was on the other side. He explained that he had seen my car in the lot and dropped in to see what I was doing. After a brief exchange, he went on his way, leaving behind the distinct impression of a dedicated leader. I admired his passion for the job and defined my own path based in no small part on his solid example.

As my responsibilities and exposure grew, I began to feel restless. My gut told me that there was something bigger and better waiting out there for me. I sensed it, and having always trusted my instincts, I allowed my restlessness to play out and see what came my way. It came as no surprise when an old friend, who was now a headhunter based out of Tampa, Florida, called me one day and said, "ABC Home Health Services, a nationwide home health agency based in Brunswick,

Georgia, is having significant problems with Medicare. Are you interested?"

Opportunity had knocked before, and now it was phoning. I quickly informed my friend that I was willing to explore it further.

Next stop: Brunswick, Georgia.

CHAPTER 3: BRUNSWICK STEW

In August of 1993, I flew to Georgia to interview with ABC Home Health Services. I was immediately offered the job and, upon my return to Florida, Columbia/HCA countered with a higher-paying position. In my interview, I had listened for keywords that suited my personality and would support my professional direction. The interviewer had explained that the job was "high pressure, fast-paced" and in need of a "go-getter." Considering what I would be leaving behind—the pressure cooker that was Columbia / HCA—ABC would be a walk in the park and provide me with a fresh professional opportunity. As I weighed the options, I felt that ABC seemed like a forward move toward self-employment. A month later, my belongings stuffed into the back of my car, I drove into Brunswick ready to begin my new, "fast-paced" adventure.

Or so I thought.

As I pulled off of the Interstate and headed into town, all I could see around me was marsh. I had two immediate thoughts: "Where the hell am I?" and "What have I done?" One week into Brunswick life, I felt like Oliver Douglas from the 60s sitcom *Green Acres*—all I was missing was a pair of overalls and a pitchfork. Brunswick's social pace was so slow, time seemed to stand still. This would have been a pro rather than a con had I been looking to retire. But obviously, I was not at that stage in my life. I didn't want to feel like it took two hours to watch *60 Minutes*, and yet, it seemed like that was the case. So, to keep occupied, I focused on work.

At ABC, I discovered a different dynamic than what I was accustomed to. While in the past I had the pressure cooker team that understood the demands of the tasks presented, at ABC I encountered a bit of a motivational challenge. I was in the office by 6:30 a.m., whereas my co-workers did not show up until 9 a.m. But, I reminded myself, I was in Hooterville now, and I had to learn the culture and adjust to the ways.

Working at ABC meant spending a great deal of time in meetings—meetings about anything and everything. Someone has a question about something? Call a meeting.   Someone doesn't understand a memo? Call a meeting. Someone has to use the restroom? Call a meeting.

At ABC, I learned the power of executing effective memos. When I couldn't get answers from the people who needed to provide them, I took my own route to finding resolutions. While at Columbia/HCA I learned that gripes from corporate didn't feel good, at ABC I learned that drawing the attention of a CEO to a matter of concern made things happen—*fast*. It's not that I liked doing things on a big scale; it's just that I wanted to get things done. Most people do not always expect things to actually be completed. I'm not that type of person. If it's on my list or caught on my watch, it will be addressed.

Once, there was a situation in which one of my memos addressed a financial matter that required immediate attention. When the recipient of the memo ignored my requests for discussion, I continued to inquire. After numerous unreturned phone calls and messages, I addressed the situation with those who needed to be informed, and that included the CEO. Suddenly, the seas parted, my calls were returned, and with that parting came the Director of Internal Audit, Bruce Hayden, right to my office door. Talk about a grand entrance.

"Welcome to Brunswick, Capullo."

Hayden proceeded to warn me about not rocking the boat with disruptive memos (translation: any memo that he wasn't interested in addressing). He explained that ABC had a protocol for handling such issues and that I had violated it.

I pleaded my case. I explained the numerous calls, the matter in question and the potential liability of the unaccounted for spending, and I gently reminded him that my job was in relation to the reconciliation of such information. He heard me out and then went back and told the Senior Vice President and Chief of Staff, Bill Stewart, of my reasoning.

What I did not know at the time of my explanation, and maybe that was a good thing, was that Hayden had actually been sent to my office to relieve me of my duties. Bill Stewart had asked him not only inform me of the existing escalation protocol, but to also show me the door. However, Hayden had found my argument and supporting reasons to be compelling and accurate, and instead returned to Bill and informed him that he could not fire me, since my reasons for escalating the complaint were well founded. From that point forward, I didn't have issues with returned phone calls or people answering my inquiries. They understood that I was there to do my job.

Jack In the Box

From my experience with the CPA firms, I had learned how important it was to be in the right work environment. As a result, after my year with ABC, it was clear to me that the job was no longer a comfortable fit for me. In 1994, I turned in my thirty-day notice. My supervisor asked if I would be willing to spend my remaining days helping ABC's CPA firm (was I ever going to stop being an accountant?) answer a pending request. The request was from the U.S. Department of Health & Human Services Office of Inspector General (OIG) in Atlanta.

Essentially, the OIG wanted ABC to produce supporting documentation for $22 million of operating costs, or return that amount of money to the Medicare program.

From my first day on the project, I was situated in a conference room with an OIG report that itemized the $22 million in costs. It included such things as interest expense of $1 million, a leadership conference that cost about $1 million and a laundry list of operating expenses too mundane to list at this time. (No, really, I want you to at least finish reading the chapter.) My job in all this was to substantiate it. I had thirty days and the help of one assistant to do it.

Immediately, I started digging through copies of old documents and invoices. I requested information from vendors and conducted telephone interviews to verify the data. I was on the project day and night, grinding away for thirty days, and I loved it. I felt my professional growth with every passing day. At the end of thirty days, the job was nowhere near done, so I offered to stay on as long as I could continue working on the project.

After two months of intense effort, I shipped twenty-two boxes of documentation to the OIG office in Atlanta. A week later, Jack Mills, the CEO of ABC, and a group of other executives from ABC flew up to meet with the OIG auditors in charge of the project. When the ABC executives returned, they gave me the bad news: OIG said that we had not adequately supported the costs.

To put it mildly, I went nuts.

I knew all the documentation was there. After all, I had not filled twenty-two boxes with company picnic photos and random announcements. No, I had gathered facts and supporting material. I asked Jack to grant me a trip to Atlanta to review it with the auditors. Perhaps he figured he had nothing to lose, because he agreed to it. Pam Melton, an ABC employee, accompanied me on the trip to provide me with assistance. We were to be there for one day.

Once at OIG, it didn't take me long to discover that the assigned auditor had done a less than thorough job. Some of the boxes that contained the necessary materials had not even been opened. Now, in a room full of boxes, I found myself asking the auditor, "How can you call it inadequate if you haven't even looked at it?"

The auditor just stared back at me. Our exchange went something like this:

Me: "You didn't even look at it, did you?"

Her: Blank stare.

Me again: "Did you?"

And again, like before, her response took the form of a silent stare. (It's very possible, and even quite likely, that she was thinking, "Darn, he's still here and still asking.")

My frustration called for an end to this Mexican stand-off and I finally just said, "We need to get to the bottom of this; go get your boss."

Enter Gerald Dunham, Audit Manager for OIG Region IV.

My first impression of Gerald was that he was annoyed by the whole situation (and, in turn, by me). I mean, I had just arrived at OIG, the auditor was supposed to be handling everything, and already he was being called in. Who had time for this?

I summarized the situation for Gerald by explaining that the report had said "not allowable," that the box with the information supporting why it *was* allowable was sealed, the auditor's supervisor who had signed off on it had retired, and so, that left him.

I didn't win any points with that exchange, I'll tell you that.

Gerald asked me to show him an example of the overlooked material. I gladly pointed out to him one item, opened the sealed box, and obtained the supporting documentation. His irritation was evident as he turned and asked the auditor if the contents had indeed been reviewed. I was pleased when he, too, got the silent stare treatment in lieu of a reply.   Gerald realized that the auditor had not reviewed any of the contents and that he was now involved in the audit of extensive materials.

It's fair to say that Gerald was less than amused by the situation. It didn't take much to figure that out when he turned to me and yelled, "I do not need some accountant haranguing my people!" I stood my ground and explained that I was not haranguing, but rather simply pointing out that the material had not been reviewed. While Gerald looked over the documents, another auditor who had been observing the ongoing exchange looked over at Gerald and remarked, "Well, if they didn't look at it, then we can't disallow it." And with that, he proceeded to call the auditor outside of the office. Moments later Gerald returned and asked, "OK, so what is it that you need?" I explained to him that all of the material needed to be reviewed. Given the magnitude of the submissions, Gerald inquired as to how long it would take.

From a one-day trip intended to just review "disallowed" documents, this excursion blossomed into a project that lasted a year and a half and consisted of checking all submitted materials with a fine-toothed comb. In the end, I managed to have OIG reduce disallowed costs of $22 million to $1.5 million.

To accomplish this endeavor it took patience, persistence, and dedication. For a year and a half, I traveled to and from Atlanta, living out of the Ritz-Carlton Hotel, reviewing documentation.

I recall how, after that first day and having managed to further enrage the very agency that was demanding repayment, I walked back to my hotel with Pam Melton, and all she could say was, "You almost got us thrown out! You almost got us thrown out! You realize you almost got us thrown out?" And each time my reply was, "But I didn't. We'll be OK." And although I was frazzled by what had happened in that initial meeting, I knew that the truth was on my side and the facts were there to back us up. When I met with Gerald again, I made sure to apologize for my tone during our initial meeting. I explained that I was just trying to do my job and represent my client. Gerald was gracious and professional. He let me know that he understood and that he had already moved on.   I realized that he was focused on his job, not his emotions. I took a big lesson from his reaction and his behavior and used it to influence my own.

Gerald was extremely accommodating throughout my entire stay. He always made himself accessible and open for discussion. We worked together when issues would arise over operating costs and whether the costs were directly related to patient care.   His approach to all the material was one of objectivity and professionalism.

One day, while having lunch in the Federal Employees' Cafeteria, he mentioned that he planned to retire in a couple of years. I made a mental note to call and congratulate him when that time came. On the day of his retirement, I telephoned Gerald's office. I found a farewell message on his office line and decided to track him down.

Gerald has worked with me for ten years since that initial meeting. In addition to his calm demeanor, he offers unparalleled auditing experience and inside knowledge on the inner workings of the government. Aside from being an amazing auditor, Gerald's input and wealth of knowledge enhances everything he participates in. His unique perspective on the healthcare system and how Medicare pays continues to amaze me.

Show Me the Money!

During the year that I handled virtually all of the OIG's requests to ABC through their CPA firm, I managed to establish myself as a Certificate of Need (CON) Expert in Alabama, Georgia, North Carolina and Tennessee. As a CON expert, I assisted in demonstrating how the creation of a new home health agency could be completed in a cost-effective manner and to the benefit of the state.

I worked days, nights and weekends, and yet my annual salary was a pittance compared to the benefit the firm received. I was aware that it billed ABC more than $1 million per year. Something was seriously wrong with my salary picture—I was worth more than what I was being paid.

When I told one of the partners in the firm that I wanted a greater piece of the benefits, he asked what I would do if he refused. I advised him I would then give it a go on my own. His answer was, "Fine, good luck to you on that. Maybe we'll throw you some of our scraps."

His words propelled me toward creating my own success. I felt I deserved more, and I was going to do what was necessary to get it.

Driven to make the most out of the situation, I took a chance and phoned Jack Mills. I remember saying to him, "Jack, this is Tony, can I talk to you?" Jack replied with his own question. "Do you drink beer?" He agreed to meet with me one day after work.

When the day came, I waited for Jack to show, my heart pounding. Here I was, meeting with Jack to make my pitch for my own consulting contract. If he refused, I would either need to find a new job or crawl back to my CPA friends with my tail between my legs. I wasn't about to do the latter, so once again, I found myself with no Plan B. However, I was not ready to settle anymore; after all, I knew I could do the work. I had been successfully doing it for someone else, why not for me? All I had to do was give the facts: I wanted to work for myself.

When Jack sat down, I explained the situation. "For the past year, I have been doing all the OIG work. I feel that I am not being adequately rewarded and"—deep breath—"I'd rather deal directly with you." It seemed pretty simple once stated. Jack stared at me, his arms crossed for what seemed like a full minute. Then he said, "I think everyone should be self-employed. All right, I agree. I'll have someone call you tomorrow." Then he added, "What would your billing rate be?"

Without really thinking about it, I blurted out, "Fifty-five dollars per hour." I quickly figured that working full-time at that rate would produce about $110,000 a year in salary. His next question baffled me. He asked, "Do you think that's fair?" I replied in earnest that yes, I thought that was fair. He then smiled and said, "Son, be careful who you're being fair to. How about $95 per hour?" Done. Jack then stood up, shook my hand, and left.

I remained seated at the table for a few minutes, pinching myself. I don't know how long I sat there. I realized I had left my comfort zone. It took a few more minutes for what had transpired to sink in. I had entered into a situation hoping for the best and had come out with more than I had expected. That moment it became clear to me that fear did not live in me.

CHAPTER 4: THE PERFECT MISFIT

Believing in myself enough to take the risk of presenting ABC with an ultimatum and the leap of faith that compelled me to call Jack and lay my cards on the table, along with the result—landing my very first client, and a significant one at that—was a pivotal period in my life. It wasn't just a professional turning point, but a personal one as well. I had known all along that I was industrious and productive and that my standards for thoroughness were exceptional, because it was my decision from the start of my working life that I would tolerate nothing less from myself. But having been boosted by Jack's acceptance of my proposal and complimented by his offer of an unsolicited increase in my fee—obviously, because he believed I was worth it—I now felt I could let other constraints that I had allowed to be put on me by the "businesss world" drop away and be my organic self. It had become clear to me now, though I had always known deep down, that it's the work that pays off, whether I am wrapped in an Armani suit and Cole Haan wingtips or a pair of Levis and a Gators T-shirt. An image is just an illusion, and it has nothing to do with the authenticity of me as an expert at what I do in business. Once I knew I could embrace this reality, I was relieved beyond measure.

There were instances, at first, however, when I wondered whether the dressed-down version of me might cause angst to others in situations where I would be representing or reflecting on them, whether it be as a consultant, expert or even as a dad. Let me explain.

When my daughter Katie was seven, she invited me to go to her school to be a teacher's assistant for a day. Her school was in a rather conservative area, and the faculty represented that conservatism. Having taken this into consideration, I spent a few days thinking about how I should dress. I knew this was important to her and so I didn't want to embarrass her.

The day before I was to be at the school, Katie said, "Daddy, I need to ask you something." She paused, then asked, "What are you going to wear?"

"What would you like me to wear?" I asked.

"Well, I really need you to wear your earrings, because I told all my friends that you're really cool."

And so I did. As it turned out, my tentativeness in this particular situation was unfounded. The kids loved my earrings and my tattoos. In the classroom I had a line of little boys ready to arm-wrestle. And, as I had expected, the teacher watched in horror. I went from being "Katie's father" to a show-and-tell project. I enjoyed every minute of it and hoped to have given a new view on the depth of appearances.

When I was a child, I wanted to be a businessman and wear suits and ties. Now that I *am* a businessman, my preferred attire is blue jeans, casual shirt, flip-flops and ball cap. I despise wearing suits and ties. But, as the owner of a business that deals with major healthcare organizations and pharmaceutical manufacturers, I can't always wear what I want when meeting with a client.

I hear it all the time when I first meet someone in a business setting: "You're not what I expected." In my occupation, it's not unusual to speak to people on the telephone several times prior to actually meeting them in person. In fact, sometimes I do business with clients for *years* without meeting them face-to-face. During that time, they invariably form a mental impression of what I look like. And when we finally do meet for the first time, they're often surprised.

It's not my intention to surprise or shock people. I'm respectful. I wear a coat and tie to all the meetings with my clients. And I certainly do not show up copping an attitude. Perhaps it's the mixture of my shaved head and physical build that make people wonder what I am about. But in reality, both are related to ease of functionality.

I started shaving my head when my forehead and my collar started to meet in the back. My hair was always naturally thick and wavy, and in South Florida's heat and humidity, that's a hellish combination to try and keep manageable. The solution: shave it.

And so, this is me: earrings, tattoos, physically fit and driven.

Beyond Appearances

So, why all this talk about appearances? Because I have found that the issue of appearance relates to the bigger issues of individuality, passion and success (however you have come to define success). And these issues help you go in your needed direction.

If you're true to yourself and you dare to be different, some people may take offense. They may even try to insult you. You need to be able to deal with the criticism. If criticism bothers you, perhaps that is because it strikes a nerve and something you may have thought true of yourself in the past. Adjust your feelings about it and take action to remedy what made you uncomfortable. And remember, as in other areas of life, it's not what happens to you, but how you deal with what happens to you that matters.

My friend Sal is a veteran Miami-Dade Homicide Detective. I met him while working out at Gold's gym. Day after day, Sal comes face-to-face with some of the most dangerous criminals in the country—"real leg-breaking troublemakers," as he calls them. One day, while sitting at Starbucks he confessed, "T, when I first saw you in the gym with all those tattoos and that shaved head, I thought you were one of those street-savvy thugs." We both laughed and I shared with him that this was a usual assumption by people judging me by my appearance. I have come to accept that assumption and move on from it.

Plain and simple, I believe that people respond to you according to how you see yourself. Because of that, I understand that being true to myself means being true to what I feel works for my personality and me. My appearance is part of that package and I have to be comfortable with myself in order to expect others to be comfortable with whom I am. I remember one situation where someone's possible lower perception of himself motivated him to attack my image. While working at a client's office, I was approached by another firm's associate asking to speak with me. I agreed to meet with him, figuring this was a client matter. In our meeting, he proceeded to tell me that certain people were making derogatory comments about my appearance. This was troubling to him, and so, in an effort to stop the comments, he was going to let me know what I should do. His advice: grow my hair, change my glasses, and cover up my tattoos. Huh?

While I found the report suspect, I wanted to ensure that I had not offended or violated any dress code policies. "Business casual" was the required attire and I had made sure to adhere to my client's policy. What's more, I didn't want any consequences of my appearance to spill over to my team. And so I spoke with my associates, who included Gerald, and everyone laughed. They assured me that nothing had been said to them and that they had not heard any comments of that kind about me. I figured the next thing to do was contact the CEO and confirm that my appearance was not an issue.

I sat with the CEO and explained to him what had been conveyed to me. He laughed and asked me why I was concerned. I advised him that the matter was brought to my attention and I wanted to make sure that I was not in any type of violation. After chuckling at the story a bit more, he proceeded to ask me who had brought the "matter" to my attention.   Before I could answer, he asked if it was a particular individual. Once he clarified who the source of the statement was the CEO enjoyed a few more chuckles. Noting that I was really touching base to ensure clarity, he advised that this was just the way this person was about things. He assured me that I had nothing to worry about. I left his office having put the gentleman's "suggestions" far behind me.

What is funny about this is, a few weeks later, I found out that this same individual had taken up working out. Who knows, by now he has probably shaved his head and considered a few tattoos of his own.

I was 18 years old when I got my first tattoo, of a panther. The story behind it is the typical "guy wants to impress girl" kind of thing. The "girl," however, was 17 years older than me and, well, you can imagine—a man's gotta do what a man's gotta do. If anything, it made for an interesting road trip. My parents never inquired as to why I got the first tattoo until years later.

About 16 years after my first tattoo I recall having a conversation with my father that comprised different topics and perspectives. It was during this time that I asked him if he had ever thought of getting a tattoo himself. He said he never had, but wondered how many of them I planned on getting. I told him that I didn't know, that it was just something that came at me once in a while. He asked what had motivated me to get the first one to begin with, and I happily shared with him the story of the road trip, the older woman who found tattoos sexy, and, needless to say, my driving teenage hormones. My father was not a man who openly discussed sex or sexual topics with his kids. About the time I alluded to the "sexy tattoo" and "hormones," he quickly interrupted with, "I don't want to hear anymore." To which I chuckled and then enjoyed a good laugh when from the adjoining room we heard my mother call out, "I heard that!"

Since that first tattoo, I have added several others. They are all for fun and because I like them. There are no hidden meanings, no silly stories, just something I saw that I liked. I find that accepting what you like and not being afraid to do what feels right for you is important in aligning with yourself. You have to be passionate about you and what you like. You can't try to become someone else's idea of who you are or who you should be. For one, you won't know the full extent of that idea and you are bound to fail trying. When you walk a walk that is not your own, or try to fit an appearance that was not created by you but by the expectations or standards of others, it is bound to be one long, tiresome and unfulfilling walk. When we are young and trying to formulate our images, we are all easily influenced. It is during that period of our lives that we figure out what we like and what we don't. In the end, you have to be happy with yourself and your personal drives to develop who you are and how you want to be.

Beyond Popularity

I feel that many people are afraid to get out of their comfort zones; whatever they may be. Most people do not want to appear different because they're insecure about what others will think. They're afraid to speak up and say what's really on their minds, perhaps because they do not want to stir up controversy. They may be lacking the courage of their convictions. For me, courage is the will to go on, in spite of fear. I have found that to overcome fear, you have to just face it.

I often tell friends, "Don't try to be different if you're not prepared to deal with the consequences." Some individuals are threatened by people who are different from them. In some cases, they even react in negative and hostile ways. But you have to be sure about you; who you are and what you do, in order to have a better take on them.

My clients' primary concern is not my appearance. What they care about are the results of my work. And just as my work experiences helped me formulate what I wanted and didn't want in a job, my alignment to my true self has given me the strength to be me. And thank goodness, because the alternative—tailoring my life to meet the expectations and desires of others—would undoubtedly limit success in all areas of my life, and guarantee failure in many. This principle holds true for every one of us as individuals, including you.

I am convinced that people are most successful when they use their unique talents to fulfill their individual dreams. To do so, they must follow their inimitable styles. I know, from my own experience, that when I tried to play a role that didn't jibe with who I am, I was unhappy and miles away from feeling like I was working toward my success. Once I aligned myself to my true desires, it was nonstop.

I don't let people's reactions bother me. When the bartender asked me if I was in the band, I thought it was hilarious. On the occasions when a person has made a negative comment about my appearance, I chalk it up to my belief that they wish he could allow himself the same freedom to be himself that I enjoy. I consider that brand of criticism a back-handed compliment.

Beyond Security

I know a number of people who are working at jobs they hate. They've become so comfortable collecting a regular paycheck that they're afraid to take risks. So instead, they daydream about what they'd rather be doing. Some of those same people have asked me, "If you could do anything in the world, what would you do?" My answer is always, "I'm doing it!"

I don't daydream about what I'd rather be doing. When the day comes that I catch myself daydreaming, I'll quit what I am doing and start doing what I was daydreaming about. There is no way around it: You have to love what you do. But even more importantly, you have to be comfortable in your own skin to do it successfully.

The most successful people are those who love what they do. There is no way to mask your excitement about something you believe in, are passionate about and driven by. It is my belief that every business is a reflection of its owner. Your energy serves as a loudspeaker for your business. That energy is your confidence, your image, your attitude. If my personality didn't match my work ethic, my business wouldn't work. If I were not comfortable in my own skin, I would still be an accountant. By being who I am, leading by my own beliefs and foundations (thus being true to myself), I allow others to be free about who they are.

In my years as a businessman, I have learned that being comfortable with who I am doesn't mean I have to become complacent about what I do. I keep challenging myself to do more and experience more. Challenges and experiences take all of us to another level.   I strive to encourage those around me to do the same, face their challenges and reach for more than what they currently are (if they desire it).

We are all unique individuals with particular gifts, talents and ideas to offer the world. We can all be more passionate, energetic, creative, productive and successful when we connect to the inner person we were intended to be. Trusting alignment to ourselves can help us put away our worries over appearances and judgments. The key is not to operate based on what others say and focus on your successful path.

For your alignment to happen, you must become acquainted with yourself first. Know your core values, beliefs, and visions. Once you find those answers (established your foundation), run your life and/or business. I know this works because I have done it, and I live it every day. In the end, it's important that you find your own rhythm and stick to it.

Convictions are powerful and your convictions determine a portion of your actions. For me, if something is not in alignment with my primary aim, I won't do it. Can this apply to you and how you base your decisions and choices? While most of my clients don't care what I look or dress like, my appearance has never cost me business. This is proof that what makes a difference is being yourself. Trust that you can have drive, ambition, focus, brains and talent and not look like the expected cookie-cutter businessman, and in the end, if your results are what they are, you'll have fun with the reactions you get and hearing the perceptions people created.

CHAPTER 5: GOING FOR THE GOALS

If someone tells me that they want to be rich or that they want to be successful, I ask them:

- What does "rich" mean to you in terms of dollars?

- What does "successful" mean to you in terms of goals?

Everyone's definitions or "rich" and "successful" are different, and, when setting goals, it's extremely important to be clear with yourself on what it is you are working toward.   If not, you are really just pointing in a direction and hoping the wind does not shift your positioning.

I'll share with you a good example of unclear desires. One day a friend asked me what I thought he should be doing with his life. I replied, "I don't know. What do *you* want to do?" "Well," he replied, "I kinda want to do this, or, I kinda want to do that." Kinda? That's not clarity. It's like being "kinda" pregnant. It's just not a true state. If you don't have clarity, you'll wind up in what I call no-man's land, the place where you sit idle and wait for things to happen around you in order for you to then react to them and hopefully have it work out.

A successful person knows what he wants. He's clear about where he's going and has an idea of how he plans to get there. He drills down with intention until he gets pinpoint clarity. I feel that's where the power is—in the intention to find it. When I sit down and face a perceived (or, at times, real) obstacle, I am determined to find the direction that I need to take in order to overcome it. I seek that greater clarity by facing the obstacle and finding possible solutions. I have found that I have more power in the clarity of a situation or goal than taking the vague stand of "kinda" for a solution or desired result.

Knowing what you *don't* want can help clarify what you *do* want. For me, my experience as an accountant and hearing the conversations of my colleagues reinforced my belief that I was just not cut out for such a direction. I then took the time to seek and, again, directly experience what came into better alignment with me. When someone says, "I don't really know what I want," I ask, "Well, what *don't* you want?" When I ask this question it seems that people think in the direction of what will bring them personal success. They focus on what they *do* want and obtain more clarity. It's the first step in making a decision and a choice based on what they have already experienced and know they do not want to repeat. I believe that their focus is shifted to taking action toward what they now desire.

Goal setting is an incremental process made up of a series of necessary steps. By knowing where I wanted to go, and having defined what I considered to be successful to *my* life, I was able to better define the necessary steps to reach my goal. I'll admit that when I started defining steps I didn't always know what the next one would be (or if it would be the right one), but when faced with decisions and business choices, I always thought out the direction in which a choice would take me. I often asked myself, "Does this choice bring me closer to my finish line, or does it cause me to drastically detour from my desired results?" Without the clear goal and understanding of what I wanted, I would not have been able to make a clear decision.

Early in my career, I knew I didn't want the stress of financial pressures. I didn't want to worry about my phone being cut off or not having gas in my car. My dissatisfaction with my financial situation drove me toward financial success. My professional goal was to achieve a comfortable lifestyle. As I mentioned, I didn't know how I was going to do it; all I knew was that my dissatisfaction with my accounting career became a powerful motivator. Have you ever noticed how, when they get frustrated enough about something, people will finally spring into action? If you're at a point in your life where you're frustrated, congratulations. Dissatisfaction is a gift; use it to propel you toward a positive goal.

Alignment

Your goals should be aligned with who you are and where you're aiming to go. They should reflect what *you* want for your life, what's right for you—*not* what you think someone else wants for your life. My parents wanted me to be an accountant; I wanted to go to St. Thomas. I returned home with a better awareness of what I wanted for myself.

You can have goals that sound wonderful, but if they are not your own, you'll never be as successful and happy as you truly hope to be. You can have a job that pays you lots of money, but if it's not in sync with who you are, you won't be happy. On occasion, I've been presented with "professional" advice, such as a business idea that may have a significant profit potential. While I always appreciate others' desire to help, I evaluate whether or not the suggestion matches my goals. If it doesn't, I don't take it. I remain true to myself and to my vision, and I recognize that while the idea may be a good one, it is probably better intended for the person giving it or for someone else. If it is not in alignment with where I'm going, it's not intended for me. This is the power of clarity.

My clarity of goals and vision is the key to running my business. In some instances, I have turned away potential clients because their goals and visions are not a direct match to my business. I have had clients ask for Professional Provider Services to do things that do not result in compliance but instead, avoid compliance. In those instances, my business model helps me to be clear and consistent on our business intentions. Professional Provider Services is about resolving potential issues and facing the challenges head on, similar to how I lead my life and business dealings.

As you can see, alignment and clarity are two concepts that hold importance and generate energy and passion in my life. When I wrote my personal philosophy, I was sure to include them:

> I live the life of my dreams every day. My energy and passion come from my self-alignment and clarity. I'm passionate about helping people and being a leader in the world. I strive to be the best I can be in everything I do. I have fun on a daily basis. I'm always smiling.

I utilize this statement as a daily reminder of the life I lead and the person I am. To ensure that I am constantly reminded of my vision, I have taped the passage above my desk.   There is no way I can miss it. I refer to it often and contemplate its message and meaning.

Overcoming Obstacles

Most people have created psychological obstacles that they may not be fully aware of, and yet, these obstacles limit their success. Some common self-created obstacles include not believing in one's own full potential, blaming the past for what's going on in the present, and the fear of failure and the embarrassment it can cause.

A good friend of mine and I were once having a conversation about dating. He was telling me how attracted he was to a certain woman. "Why don't you ask her out?" I asked him. He replied, "Oh, she wouldn't go out with me." In his mind, he was defeated even before he had made an attempt. Here was an obvious disconnect between what he wanted and what he thought he could have. He was paralyzed by the fear of failing.

You must not allow yourself to be afraid to fail. In life, people who are unwilling to take risks seldom reap worthwhile rewards. Taking risks is part of what it takes to be successful. It's part of the journey. Your journey does not start by sitting in the same place. In my opinion, it starts in the mind. Mental attitude is 80 percent of the battle, which means your mindset is 80 percent in your favor or your detriment.

Many people don't pursue their heartfelt goals because they've consciously or subconsciously decided that they can't attain them. They focus on the potential problems they will encounter instead of the potential payoffs they will enjoy. They think about the discomforts they will experience while striving for their goals instead of the rewards they will enjoy after achieving their goals. In every job I've held that called for long hours and continuous challenges, I endeavored to focus my attention not on the negative aspects of the job, but on the desired outcome and the rewards of that outcome. In some situations, it was the proper completion of the task. In others, it was the potential for professional growth. And in the end, it was the desire for self-employment. I don't claim that this was an easy road. But that's only because I have viewed it as enjoyment rather than difficulty. My mind has been 80 percent in favor of the experience and not the potential of defeat.

It's my experience that people who are afraid of failure often have trouble setting goals. Goal setting requires knowing what you want and the act of setting goals may bring out a mental obstacle in the individual. This obstacle is the realization that he does not really know what he wants. And so, to avoid the pain of disappointment, he may bury his true desires so deeply that he loses touch with the desire *and* himself.

Many years ago, I had difficulty setting my goal for my future. I knew that in the end I desired to be self-employed. I had no intention of losing touch with that desire; I just didn't know how I would get there. But I wanted it badly. I remember seeking assistance on the how-to by listening to a motivational tape of Tony Robbins (you know, the really tall guy). On it, Robbins asked, "What would you do if you knew you could not fail?" Taking the time to think about that question and to truthfully answer it helped me move past the imagined block, the one that kept telling me, "I don't know how I'll get there." It helped me find answers and potential actions to move me toward my goals.

As you overcome your self-generated fears, you need to learn to have belief. Belief is the driving force of achievement. You have to believe you *can* achieve your goals before you actually achieve them. Think about that for a moment. If you have an idea but you really don't think it will materialize, what are the chances that it will? Remember, your mental attitude is 80 percent of the result.

I have an incredibly strong belief system. Whatever I set my mind to *is* going to happen. I'm not bragging; it's what I believe to be true. And by believing it to be true, it is. It's that simple. My method is even simpler: I talk myself into it. I plant a positive thought in my mind and it grows into good and greater things. The only way my mind knows any different is if I tell it that it won't happen. And why the hell would I do that when it's something that I want? My mind just does its job and assumes my thoughts are facts, and in turn generates fresh ideas and possible actions that help me reach my goals.

I have been in many situations where my knee-jerk reaction was, "There's no way I can do that." It's natural. Like I said, moving out of the comfort zone is never easy. But in the end, you just have to do it. In those situations, where moving out of the comfort zone proved more difficult than others, I learned the power of self-talk. I remember in one instance having to explain to a group of high-level defense attorneys how a client's action caused minimal damage to the Medicare program and that this was key information they could present to the government. My input was integral to their defense. No pressure whatsoever, right?

Prior to meeting with the attorneys, I had a severe case of the jitters. I knew my information had to be clean, accurate and detailed, with the necessary supporting facts; this meant my nerves had to be left in another room. The attorneys were counting on me to provide them with necessary information on a criminal case. I felt like *The Little Engine That Could*, sitting in my room talking myself out of the nerves and worry. It's like a performer preparing to step out onstage: even though he knows he's talented, all eyes are going to be on him, and how he delivers is crucial. Pressure.

The trick was to change my focus from *whom* it was I was presenting to, to *what* I was presenting. I had to get past my perceptions of not being able to do it by telling my mind that I could. By changing my focus to the necessary facts, I worked my way past the butterflies.

Interestingly enough, once the presentation was in full swing, a prominent but caustic defense attorney who was present, flippantly interrupted me with, "You couldn't come up with anything better than that?" Had I not been able to work through my pre-presentation uncertainty, I might not have been able to answer him as I did: "Listen, unless you want to do this yourself, let me finish." He later apologized, and in the end they went with my strategy.

Self-talk is a powerful personal tool that is accessible to all of us. However, we are more accustomed to using self-talk negatively than as the beneficial tool it should and can be. We spend more time verbalizing our fears of possible hardships and our perceived inability to reach a goal than telling ourselves about our true ability to complete it. For me, self-talking is an indispensable tool that I use to reinforce my desires versus work toward defeating them.

I believe everyone should think big. Set goals that are inspiring, so when you think about them, they excite the hell out of you and engage you in positive self-talk. Reach beyond the familiar. The best goals will stretch you and make you a little uncomfortable. If you're making $50,000 a year and make it your goal to start earning $200,000, that's exciting! Don't sit there and think, "Oh, man, that's going to take a lot of work; maybe I should just aim for $75,000." Remember, it's your goal, and the rewards will be magnificent once you reach it.

By thinking positive, you give yourself more momentum. When you allow negative thoughts to take precedence in your mind, you're just throwing obstacles in your path and delaying your pace to the desired goal. And rest assured, obstacles *will* pop up at times without your help, so avoid placing any in your own path.

Oh, I know, it sounds simplistic when negative thoughts have always been predominant for you, or you've had a disappointing past. Such a history makes it tough to say, "I think I can, I think I can." But remember, the only thing you can control is your mind. And whatever you feed it, it will eventually believe if you say it often enough and with *enough conviction*. Try it. I don't mean try it for a day. Try it over an extended period of time. It works.

I have found that the biggest rewards and the most excitement come when I step outside of my comfort zone. If thinking positive is outside of yours, then you are in for a wonderful ride once you decide to start. And by the way, when I get outside of my comfort zone, my physiology changes: my mouth goes dry, my heart races and my breathing patterns change. That's when I know I'm on the right track and great things are about to happen.

The Mighty Pen

When someone tells me they have "a lot of goals," I often ask them where those goals are stored. Usually, they point to their heads and reply, "Up here." Well, that's nice, but I wonder if they realize that they're missing out on a reservoir of untapped power: WRITING.

At any given time, on any given day, there's so much going on around us for any of us to keep our goals "up here," in our heads. Writing down your goals forces you to focus on what you want.

I am going to share with you what I have done that has worked for me.

1. To tap into your power reservoir, the first thing to do is to sit down and start to write. Ask yourself these questions:
    - What's the goal?
    - What's the objective?

    Get a clear picture in your mind of what you want. You don't have to have a clue about how you will achieve it. Don't worry about strategies or action steps. Just start writing about what you want. Every little step is progress.

2. Write down why you want to achieve this goal. Why is it important? How will you feel when you achieve it? No one pursues goals for the sake of pursuing goals. We do it to gain rewards. Identify those rewards. Figure out what drives you.

3. Engage your emotions. Create mental pictures that stir up your feelings and get you excited. Emotions fuel goals! When your feelings aren't involved, goal setting becomes simply a mechanical process. But when your feelings are driving you, goals are powerful! Write out your emotions as you describe your goals.

    One of my goals is to someday receive a single check for $1 million. I don't know when it will happen, but it will. The other day, I found the image of a check on the Internet and doctored it to look like the one I want to receive, complete with the name of my company. Then I printed it and put it in my book of goals. That visual increases my drive to achieve that goal.

4. Set a goal date. Goals should be measurable, so you'll know when you achieve them. Specify the end result and the completion date as clearly as possible. I have some goals that

are ongoing, such as to be a good parent; there is no end date for that one. However, most of my goals have definite completion points. Identify yours.

5. Know what you *think* you may face (you will discover that these are really the fears that are holding you back). Anticipate the potential obstacles you might encounter as you work toward your goals and list the possible solutions for overcoming those obstacles. The process of listing the obstacles gives you confidence because you're squarely facing them. Anticipating obstacles also lets you plan ways around them. Sometimes anticipated obstacles don't become real obstacles. But if they do, you have a plan.

6. Write down the rewards you expect to receive when you accomplish your goals, and the consequences you will experience if you don't achieve them. Focusing on rewards and consequences will get you excited. It will give you a motivational boost that will help you persevere through difficulties.

7. Develop your plan. List the action steps you need to take to accomplish your goals and start taking action. Think it through. I'm a strong believer in preparation. Don't leave anything to chance. Write your plan; work your plan.

    Remember, you have to be flexible. Adjust as you go. Don't just write something down and blindly plow ahead. Sometimes the environment will change, or the people will change. Sometimes you'll run into obstacles you didn't anticipate, so even though a plan is crucial, always be open to adjustment.

    Take a cue from the great football coaches. If they have a bad first half, they'll adjust their game plan for the second half. If what you're doing isn't working, you probably don't need to change your goal, but you will need to develop a different strategy.

8. Devote time to your vision. Some people write down their goals and never look at them. Don't make that mistake. Spend fifteen to thirty minutes focusing on your goals at least two to three times a week. Repeated review of your goals increases clarity and commitment and generates new ideas for action.

Storing goals in your head is not the same as having them in writing. The process of writing forces clarity and adds conviction. Plus, when your goals are in writing, you can refer to them and focus on them. Writing your goals doesn't guarantee success, but it sure increases the probability of success. The act of writing forces you to focus on what you want, how you are going to feel when you get there, why you want it, and then your thoughts lead you to come up with a strategy to get there. It's *all* about clarity.

When I first started my business, my goal was to be self-employed. In order to do that, I needed a client. I couldn't just hang out a shingle and expect to start a business, so securing a client became a sub-goal within my main goal of starting a business.

My first action step was to approach Jack Mills, (ABC Home Health) and ask for him for his business. When he said yes, that generated a whole series of additional action steps about office space, billing procedures and so forth. But if his answer had been "no," I would have come up with another plan and set of action steps.

This process sounds simple, and in some ways it is. But in other ways, it's not. In order to move forward, I had to overcome emotional obstacles, such as fear and apprehension. A "no" from Jack would have sent me back to square one. Having a goal and a plan allowed me to push through fear and go for what I wanted. It made all the difference.

You Must Keep Going and Going

To be successful at goal setting, you've got to be persistent. You will be told "no" many, many times. If you're not willing to be persistent and push ahead, you might as well give up now.

Most people give up way too soon. They get rejected, they don't think they're moving forward, they realize it's not going to be easy or they stumble out of the blocks, so they quit. Don't do that. **You can't quit and be successful.**

I've discovered that there's a silver lining to every dark cloud of rejection. So when I run up against an obstacle, I don't quit. I hang in there and look for a way around it. Every obstacle has a workable solution. By devoting time and thought to the situation, I can usually find a solution. Most people can, if they try.

Once when I was making a pitch to a potential client, they gave me lots of valid-sounding reasons why they didn't need my services. I was disappointed by their rejection, but I didn't get discouraged. I just kept moving forward looking for business in other places. One week later, they called and asked for my help. This client turned out to be the best and most lucrative client I've had to date.

- Where there's a "no," there's a "yes."

Even if someone tells you "no" a thousand times, that same person can still say "yes." You can never tell when circumstances will change. A door that's closed one week may open the next week. Besides, when you get rejected, you're in good company. Everyone, at some time or another, gets rejected. It is also important to remember that rejection is temporary. Someone may tell you "no" today and next week be in a different situation and ready to say "yes."

Remember how while working at the hospital during budget cuts I asked for my team to remain intact? I asked and I received. Most people are afraid to ask for what they want because they want to avoid the pain of rejection. If it weren't for the threat of pain, they'd ask. But you've got to be willing to walk through the pain. It's a choice. You can either hate the pain so much that you give up, or you can use it to drive you forward.

- There is no harm in the way of asking, only your ego.

I've been rejected so many times, I've become immune to the pain or discomfort that it causes. To me, rejections are inspiring. They make me want something more. When somebody tells me "no" or "not right now," I become more focused and more determined. I dig down deeper and try harder.

And that leads me to persistence. If two people are trying to sell me products or services that are similar, I'll buy from the one who is more persistent—not pushy—just because I figure he wants my business more. Often, persistence is equal to passion. When you want something bad enough, nothing stops you. It's a direct expression of loving what you do. To that end, some clients have said that they hired me because I persisted.

- Keep trying.

I always ask myself when I set a new goal, "What am I willing to do to make it happen? Am willing to hang myself out there? How badly do I want it?" To achieve big goals, you've got want them so much that you'll be willing to persevere and never give up. Transform each of your goals into a personal obsession.

- Be determined. Stay the course.

If you don't accomplish a goal, don't get discouraged. Regroup and start moving forward again. One thing that helps me keep my confidence up is to look back at past goals I've accomplished. This is when it really comes in handy to have written down your goals. When I look back at all the things that I've done that others told me were impossible, how can I be discouraged? I just keep moving forward to accomplish more "impossible" things.

Focusing on Goals

I've already said that you can't just set goals and expect them to just happen. You have to focus on them in such a way that you are prompted to take action. How? I don't pretend to have all the answers, but I'll tell you what works for me, and perhaps the same things could work for you.

I start my day on the focused path and spend at least thirty minutes every morning focusing on my attitude and my goals. My routine is simple: I get a legal pad, ask myself questions and write down my answers. Questions help me to focus, and writing helps me to think. There's incredible power in writing, and I tap into that power first thing in the morning. Why not? Might as well start off strong.

I have come to find that the best questions are ones that presuppose progress and success.

For example:

- What's phenomenal about today?

- How do I feel about moving closer to my goals?

These questions trick my brain into focusing on the positive. With the first inquiry, I tell myself today is great. This means I am expecting and establishing my behavior from a place of greatness in order to achieve my intended goal. The second question tells my brain we are doing everything in our power, mentally and physically, to accomplish something that moves me closer to meeting my goal. Both questions have a powerful effect on my attitude and goals. And this is why I ask them. When I ask myself these particularly pointed questions and then take the time to answer them in writing, I have no choice but to start the day fired up.

I also write questions when I'm faced with a challenge. I ask questions such as, "What's good about this situation that I didn't notice?" Then I write my answers. That helps me focus 80 percent of my attention on the solution, and only 20 percent on the problem. Because of the way I word my questions, I bring to the surface the things I may have overlooked that were conducive to continuing my forward movement. It really works.

Every day I go back and look at my goals. Am I getting closer? If not, why? Do I need to change my strategy? What else can I do to move closer to this goal? I write down all my questions and answers on a legal pad. This is the system that works for me. I've honed it through trial and error. But you should develop the system that works best for you.

At any one time, I'm working on twenty to twenty-five goals. I keep them all in a notebook. They're divided into groups, such as professional, personal, social and spiritual. They're also divided into three time categories: short-term, intermediate-term and long-term. Every goal is specific, measurable, ambitious and attainable. And most of all, I make sure they contain clarity.

All of the goals I'm currently working on are in one three-ring binder. In a separate notebook, I keep a chronological file of all of my handwritten thoughts about my goals.   Every morning, I'll add a few more pages of notes. When a notebook is filled, I put it on the shelf and start another. The shelves of my office are filled with notebooks of past goals that I've achieved. In fact, I still have my first goal notebook that dates back to 1994.

One day, a friend who was visiting me asked, "What's in all those books on your shelves?" When I told him they contained my goals, he said, "That's corny." I respected his opinion, but knew that what was corny to him is productive to me.

Incidentally, two months later that very same friend came back to see me. He confessed that he wasn't where he wanted to be in life, and he asked me to show him how to set goals.

Goal setting is about turning thoughts into reality. It is magical process, and I am forever grateful for having learned it and consistently applied it. Try it yourself.

CHAPTER 6: THE TRICKLE-DOWN THEORY

Reading the title of this chapter may call up the idea of economic policy to many of you, but there is a different trickle-down theory I subscribe to in business, and it works. The philosophy itself is simple, and certainly not one I invented: surround yourself with smart people, set the tone for them from the top of the organization, and go.

Believing in yourself and your decisions, developing a dependable team, working with an effective coach, and learning to deal with adversity—because you *will* encounter setbacks along the way, some expected and some not—are key steps to building a successful company.

When I started PPS, I was already aware that the tone of everything started with me, because I was at the top. I was determined to design a blueprint for strategic leadership. I knew I had to be tuned in to a lot of things I never had to worry about before. As the person who calls the shots, you're not always popular, but that doesn't matter—what's important is to have enough confidence in your decision to believe you're doing the right thing. Though I like and encourage a participatory environment, ultimately, it's not a democracy; it's an autocracy. Whatever result I got or didn't get was determined by the tone that I set. I didn't (and still don't) make decisions based on sentiment. I may like someone very much. However, every decision I make is made with the best interest of the company in mind. "What is best for the company? Does this move us forward toward our strategic objective?"

My first organizational chart was easy to develop because my name was in every box. But with growth came the need to build a business that extended beyond just me. One of the basics of business school is to write a compelling vision statement. That was no mean feat, either, because I had a crystal clear vision of what I wanted the company to be, what services I wanted to provide and the caliber of people I needed to have working with me. The next step, however, wasn't so simple—to make the vision a reality: assemble the quality team and strategy I needed to get where I wanted to go (that would be to the top, in case you were wondering). It was key to put together a staff that could run the company without me, which is to say a business that runs on *systems*. When systems are in place and everyone understands them and what has to be done, it frees me up to focus on more important issues, and I'm able to get work done through others.

This is crucial, because as the boss I have to be able to pay attention to the long-term objectives and not get mired in the short-term issues. Too often, small companies become addicted to short-term successes. And while the potential to over-manage sometimes becomes a reality, as a general rule you have to focus on the future. As difficult as it can be, worrying about today and tomorrow simultaneously without sacrificing your long-term objectives is a balancing act that must be mastered. To do this successfully requires intuition, creativity and planning. I pride myself on having good intuition; your gut feeling is a gift that mustn't be ignored, regardless of what anyone else tells you.

Hiring Great People

In addition to being good at their jobs, your staff must be committed. A Harvard MBA is nothing more than a piece of paper if the candidate for the job doesn't share your drive and your goals for the company, and ideally, great strength in an area that is not your field of expertise.

And no one person can make or break the organization. You may set your sights on adding a certain person to the company, but if you convince yourself that you need a certain individual to reach your goals, you have already lost. One person can have an impact but there is no one who can make up for inherent weaknesses in your organization, a foundational weakness. My goal was to build the foundation up to get to the point where I didn't need to add that one particular person.

Prior to being brought on to work on any project with PPS, potential employees are taken through a process of determining what their primary aim is and what they value most. The underlying philosophy is this: Employees must be committed to their work and do whatever it takes to get the best results in order to be part of this team. They can only do this if they see the connection between what they do at work and what they want in their lives. As the boss, I need to understand the connection for each employee as well, so that I can provide the kind of support they need to move them past their obstacles and keep them focused on their goals.

In addition to reviewing a consultant's personal goals, I explain exactly what they can expect from me, what I expect from them, and the basis of our relationship. The idea is to lay the foundation for working together and producing measurable results. My philosophy is that we'll get off to a better start by letting them know exactly what my expectations are. In addition, I also ask them what they need from me in order to be effective. In my mind, this helps establish trust and open communication from the beginning.

It also allows me to get a sense of what their triggers are. For example, certain people thrive under pressure, some don't, and learning as much as possible ahead of time helps immensely in understanding where someone will fit in the overall scheme of the organization. By knowing the character of the person you're dealing with, you'll be better able to gauge how they will perform under various circumstances; after all, if someone is going to represent the company before our clients, the last thing I want to worry about is having them—or me—look foolish.

That's why one of the things I stress adamantly to everyone on my team is: prepare, prepare, prepare. We receive an agenda before attending a conference or meeting detailing who will be there. Once we get it, we research all of them, take note of what the reporting order will be, issues up front, what are they going to talk about, if they're regulatory or statutory issues. We research them ahead of time and go armed with that information. Even if you go and you're overly prepared, there's something to be said for knowing more about your client than he knows about himself. Preparation and knowledge empowers your personnel and in turn helps them to produce more and better results.

By surrounding myself with those who know more about various aspects of my business than I do, I gain the confidence and security of knowing that PPS is equipped to compete at the highest level in the industry and, in turn, reach its goals sooner. It's the same principle in business as in sports: Better players win more games. After all, if you were coaching a baseball team, would you rather have experienced players taking the field or nine rookies? Winners bring determination, focus and an enthusiasm that's infectious. Gerald Dunham is an example of this dynamic. A former longtime high-ranking government official, he has won numerous awards for his work and is known in the industry for his stellar reputation and professional savvy. Yet he is virtually without ego and has a gift for inspiring those who work with him. During the first year of our working relationship, I was talking with Blue Cross about a potential project. As soon as I mentioned Gerry Dunham, the deal was sealed. And yet, ironically, when speaking to them, he responded to one of their inquiries with, "I'll have to talk to Tony. He's the boss." He has never referred to me otherwise, and calls me "Boss" to this day every time we speak. I am floored by the level of respect he gives me despite his many more years of experience, success and well-earned honors for his expertise.

And yet, as key as anyone may be, don't ever convince yourself that any single person is crucial to your success. *You must have a team.*

Now, having emphasized the importance of a cohesive, strong team, a successful business cannot be people-dependent. We've all been in work environments where one person either resigns or is fired, leaving everyone remaining at the company scrambling to figure out where that person's files are, what correspondence took place with clients, or at what point he or she was in the preparation of a presentation. When an individual leaves and no one knows what he or she had been doing or how to do it, that's a breakdown in the system. There must be others who are trained and ready to take over that person's job *just in case*. PPS can run smoothly without me on a day-to-day basis, whereas when I first started, a vacation was out of the question for me because I'd have heart palpitations obsessing about what might happen if I wasn't there to fix it. That sort of existence was not consistent with my original vision—I wasn't running my business; it was running me.

To get over this hurdle, I hired a business coach. The single-most important benefit I've reaped from it is a clear understanding of how my business serves to fulfill my life's primary objective. I now know how to integrate the professional and personal aspects of my life and am able to make intentional choices. By recognizing what makes a business run effectively, I became a more effective leader, managing from a position of strength. This shift led to measurable results. Whereas we once did things by hook or by crook (and fortunately got lucky more often than not), our operating philosophy went from "We'll find a way to do it" to "This is how we're going to do it." The coaching was key. It identified the gaps between where I was and where I needed to be. Strategies sometimes were not big things, just small modifications, but collectively, they were huge.

It would be reasonable for you to ask me, "Why do you need a coach if you believe in your intuition?" (Which, by the way, I always have.) I had been in business a decade before I hired a coach, and even though the company had never lost money and was, in fact, flourishing, I knew that growth was key and so I didn't want to be complacent. I wanted to get to the next level. I guess I could have sat back and enjoyed the ride, but that's not how I'm built. And when I saw the business diagnostic Jeff Burrows sent me—addressing issues of leadership, money, marketing, management, lead generation, lead conversion, client fulfillment—well, let's just say it was a sobering experience. About halfway through it, I was ready to leap off the building. Clearly, we didn't have the systems in place that were necessary for my desired growth.

And it's not just business owners who can reap the benefits of a coach's counsel. Anyone who wants to excel personally and professionally should consider this. It always pains me when I ask someone, "How are you doing?" and he responds, "I'm doing OK" or "I'm hanging in there." My answer to that is always, "Sorry to hear it." Because there's no need to be mired in that state interminably—there is always a better place. You may be good at your job, but through effective coaching you have the opportunity to become exceptional. "Doing pretty well" may be good enough for people who are stuck in the meantime, but living and working in that state forever doesn't inspire, it doesn't feed passion and it doesn't present the chance to experience the brand of all-around satisfaction that comes with knowing you're fulfilling your potential.

If I were to sell my company and work for someone else, the one thing I'd stipulate as a condition of my contract is a coach. If you want me to operate at maximum capacity and you want to take a bow at board meetings, I need a coach. Each one has his own philosophy and style, and good ones know how to bring the best out of the people they work with.

All of the things I've addressed in this chapter until this point are based partly on what I've learned through experience and from some brilliant people I've been fortunate enough to work with. But my journey to this point wouldn't have been possible without my staunch belief that I'd make it happen. Even at the worst moments— like when my phone was cut off in Fort Myers—that belief didn't waver for a moment. I don't know why, but it's true. I was willing to seek out something I loved to do and turn it into a rewarding career. How could a guy who had his credit card cut up have such an unwavering belief? I don't know. I never questioned my belief system; I just accepted it.

CHAPTER 7: ADDRESSING THE ENERGY CRISIS

Some people seem to live in a constant state of fatigue, dragging through life completely zapped of energy. They speak slowly and move even slower. They appear passionless. When the going gets tough, they don't have the stamina to keep going. They wear out before the day is done. The tough settings often leave them scared.

And then there are those who always seem to have to exude confidence and enthusiasm, even in the face of adversity. Their demeanor conveys purpose, focus and a zest for life. These are the individuals who are successful in whatever they do.

Where do these people get their drive? How is it that this group considers themselves successful? While a few are naturally energetic, sometimes they even seem to be blessed with good genes. And then there are some of us that have to work at building that confidence-filled swagger and desired physique. We either hire trainers or we focus on our desired outcome and do the necessary work to move toward our physical objective.

Until the age of two, I had a problem with my legs. To correct the problem I had to wear special shoes that had a bar across them to assist in straightening my legs. The limbs had to be trained and molded to adjust to a setting that would benefit the body as a whole. The adjusting and shaping had to be a coordinated effort of desire (that of my parents), of training (the bars), and of dedication (consistently wearing the necessary item). As an adult, I came to realize that, just as my legs needed adjusting when I was a child, in order to obtain what I desired of myself physically I needed to be deliberate about nutrition, exercise and rest.

When I was in college, my dietary staples consisted of macaroni-

and-cheese and Ramen noodles. I was your typical broke college student (which translates to: earn twenty bucks, invest it wisely at the local bar) and the right food was not a priority, so I ate what I could afford without much concern for what it did to my body. Nor did I worry about eating regular meals. You can imagine how happy I was when my part-time job as a busboy at a nearby restaurant offered not only cash, but free food.

And while I was not up for putting together a real meal on my own, with the help of my college buddy, Alan, I mastered the art of stretching a twenty-dollar bill across an entire night of drinks. It is truly incredible how, when you are young, your body has a way of compensating for your lack of logic, at least for a little while.

I was nineteen and starting my sophomore year when I noticed a drastic drop in my weight. Up to that point, I had been active and somewhat healthy (or lucky to have my health in spite of my nutritional choices), so to find myself weighing in at 130 was a bit of a surprise. Shortly after the weight loss, I became jaundiced. Unable to figure out what was wrong, I went home to my parents.

My family doctor ordered me to take a series of tests. The results showed that I had an enzyme in my blood that measured higher than normal. The doctor explained that the release of this enzyme was caused when muscles were overworked. I was puzzled. The doctor advised my parents that I needed to be still and rest. He emphasized that I was to have limited movement to avoid the triggering of this enzyme, and even went so far as to suggest that I could possibly have Multiple Sclerosis (MS).

Alarmed by the diagnosis, my parents took immediate action to enforce my prescribed rest. In record time, I had been withdrawn from my academic courses, moved out of my dormitory and placed under the care and observation of my mother, who became the Rest Enforcer.

This "sitting still" thing did not go over well with me. Aside from taking medication, I was not allowed to do *anything*. So, I did the next best thing: I drove my mother crazy pushing the limits of what I felt I *could* do. I just didn't believe I had or could have MS. I simply wouldn't accept the idea. But the situation was real, and I needed to remedy my physical state. During my quiet moments, I started reading and became a fan of *Eat to Win* written by Dr. Robert Haas. This was the first time that I had taken a serious look at my nutrition. I read the book at least twice, and, being that my movement was restricted, I asked my mother to prepare my food. For the first time in my life, I consciously shifted my diet. I started eating brown rice, lean chicken, vegetables and fruits. Little by little, my weight increased.

With the combination of rest, medication and appropriate nutritional choices, I regained my strength. Because I remained very limited to any physical activity, I found ways to escape my parents' collective watchful eye. They never objected when I would say I was going to get extra sleep, so I would close the door to my room. But instead of sleeping, I would do push-ups and sit-ups, telling myself, "There is no way I have MS if I can complete these exercises." Slowly but surely, I started building up muscle.

After a final follow-up with the doctor, I was given a clean bill of health and cleared to return to school. The MS scare was dismissed, much to the relief of my family. I went back to college with a different perspective on my health and attitude. I took time to focus on what I ate and how I treated my body. No, this did not stop me from calculating how many drinks I could buy at my favorite bar, but it did make me wiser on how to be more balanced with my choices. I couldn't give my body junk food and alcohol and expect it to perform at its optimum level. I had to create and follow a new diet, and when I came close to complaining, I reminded myself how horrible I felt being immobile and sickly during the time I'd spent at home.

When self-motivation became difficult, I looked to athletes that I admired, such as the famous Boston Red Sox catcher Carlton Fisk, and mimicked their hard work and dedication to physical fitness. I found his efforts admirable and used this inspiration to drive my new lifestyle. I simply could not allow myself to end up in the same state that I had experienced that semester. The scare and stress that the prospect of my failing health had caused my family and me cemented the need for conscious choices. To this day, I work out with that experience clear in my mind; a conscious awareness of where I do *not* want to be ever again.

Exercise: Cab Ride to Fitness

Not too long ago, as I was leaving the office after a twelve-hour day of challenges and frustrations, I felt like my brain was fried. The last thing I felt like doing was working out. It would have been incredibly easy to turn my car around and head to my favorite bar to join friends for drinks and a few laughs. Actually, that's what I would have preferred to do. I'll admit that it crossed my mind for a minute, but I mustered my self-discipline and went to the gym as usual.

Within a few minutes of being into my workout, the adrenaline was flowing, the sweat was dripping and I was completely refocused. Once I got going, I was off to the races. It's all basic physics: An object in motion remains in motion. Exercise creates that energetic momentum that is not so easy to stop.

I have found that regular exercise increases my productivity in at least three ways:

- I accomplish more because my mind is clearer and better able to focus. That enables me to move faster and get things done more quickly, yet still efficiently.

- I get more done every day because I need less sleep. The energy I generate by being fit helps me stay alert. You won't find me with my head down on my desk at two in the afternoon, trying to catch a catnap; I am too naturally revved up to need it.

- I stand to get more done over the span of my life because healthy people typically live longer.

I don't think a cup of coffee can provide such rewards.

When you are not in good physical condition, when you feel sluggish and tired much of the time, you come to experience some of following negative results:

- Productivity plummets down off a cliff;

- Aches and pains adversely affect your confidence and your outlook;

- You have trouble maintaining a positive mental attitude;

- You have less ability to accomplish your goals because you don't feel good about yourself—and you just don't feel good, period.

That is what so many Americans experience, and they wonder why. They never stop and think that maybe part of the cause is a lack of physical conditioning.

Years ago, I would be up at 2:30 in the morning, at the gym by 3:30 a.m., finished exercising by 5:30 a.m., and at the office, revved up and raring to go, by 6:30 a.m. Friends and colleagues thought I was nuts. (Hell, *I* thought I was nuts.) But I loved it. The workouts physically prepared me for the obstacles and challenges that the day would bring. While many sought their morning fix of "energy in a cup," I functioned as my own generator throughout the day. I was so pumped and ready to go that, on some days, depending on the intensity of the work out I had completed, I felt like I could walk through a wall. This feeling only reassured me of how easily I was able to endure the day.

When my daughter was born, my priorities changed. Katie was a colic baby, and that meant a number of all-nighters spent against a backdrop of bloodcurdling screams. I did the best to continue my fitness schedule but, understandably, my workouts were not as consistent or as intense as they had been before. Because I was running on little to no sleep, I found it hard to function on any level. Since my priority was my daughter and her wellness, fitness took the passenger seat until she was better adjusted.

When life calmed down and things were back to normal, I returned to a more balanced physical routine. I discovered that a good workout, aside from external physical changes, gave me a body that used rest times more efficiently.

I understand how busy we can all be and how easy it is to make a million excuses for not getting into the gym. I also know from personal experience how difficult it is to stick to an exercise routine when traveling on business. The good thing is that just about anywhere you go, you can find a health club or gym to fit your needs; it just may take a little more planning when you book your reservations. But if you take the time to look up the best restaurants in the area, or ask the front desk where to shop, you can also find the nearest workout facility, and you'll feel much better for having stuck to your plan. Many hotels offer small gyms for your convenience, and while these often resemble a phone booth with a treadmill and three dumbbells stuffed into it, they're convenient and accessible. Make it a habit to plan and research local health clubs in the city where you will be staying. Physical fitness should be every bit as important in your life as your own entertainment—more so—and giving it a place on your list of goals motivates you to make it an integral part of your daily routine.

In 2001, I was working on a project in Oklahoma City. The project lasted well over a year, so I was frequently flying back and forth, and in some cases, staying through the weekends. On one particular trip I arrived right after a massive ice storm had hit the area, and everything in town was closed, including the gym where I normally worked out while there. After speaking to the hotel's front desk, I found a gym several miles outside the city that was open twenty-four hours. I called and, to my relief, was greeted by the attendant with, "Yes, we're open."

I commandeered a cabdriver who courageously agreed to drive me over the slick and snowy roads. When I arrived, the place was empty except for the guy who had answered my call. Sitting comfortably in his chair with his feet propped up on the counter, he probably wished every night was like that particular evening. Once inside, I got to work. I completed my work out and returned to my hotel at 1:00 am.

To some, my actions that night may sound a bit obsessive. But what it did for me was achieve a feeling of accomplishment and satisfaction for sticking to my goal. You see, if I would have curtailed my workout due to the weather on that particular night, the next day it would have been easier to say it was too cold or that I was too tired; before you know it, it could have escalated to a week without a workout. In the end, I did what I wanted and had set out to do.

For me, dedication is not necessarily obsession; it's a deep desire to accomplish something. My goal was not to sit in the hotel room and watch television. My goal also didn't involve visiting a bar that evening. I had my focus and priorities. I still remember the greeting from the gym attendant when I walked in that night. He said, "Dude, you are one dedicated guy." He was right.

The Early Bird Catches the Worm

As a child, I was the early riser of the family. I made it my job to get everyone up and going. As children, we have boundless energy. We practically ricochet off the walls if given the space to do so. This is our inherent nature. As we age, we tend to slow down. When I was young, my father helped to instill the importance of an early wake-up by making my Saturday mornings our bonding time with yard work. There is no doubt that as I grew older, my desire to do my chosen activities versus battle a lawn mower definitely held a higher priority. But I learned that the earlier the yard work was completed, the more time I had to do my own things and feel accomplished. Everyone in the family was up and moving by 7:30 a.m.; otherwise, my mother woke them with her vacuuming. As a result, I embraced the message early: it isn't productive to sleep late.

I realize that I do more before breakfast than most people do in a day. Part of this is just my drive; the rest I attribute to the energy that being healthy produces. Waking early and getting my body and mind moving refreshes and motivates me. By the time most people are filing into work getting their coffee, I'm knee-deep in momentum and seizing opportunities. Being industrious brings a great feeling of accomplishment that continues to motivate and drive you toward accomplishing further goals. Try setting your alarm for an earlier wake-up time and tackling your list of to-dos a little earlier than you originally intended. You'll be amazed at how accomplished and driven you feel in comparison to your former sluggish start.

Finding the workout that's best for you and keeps you motivated is important. I have found mitts as a perfect fit for my personality and needs. Mitts is a high-velocity activity involving legs, core muscles, hips, shoulders and arms; not a single body part goes unexercised. Here's how it works: My trainer, Mark Estrada, holds up punching pads and calls out combinations for me to use to strike the pads. At times he calls for jabs, hooks or uppercuts. All of the moves emphasize hand speed and hand-eye coordination. Since he is not training me with the goal of making me a boxer, Mark emphasizes developing endurance and improved cardiovascular fitness. As a result, every part of me is engaged (mind and body) and the activity reflects the way I live my life: always engaged, always in the moment.

Mark believes in the principle of "muscle confusion." He "confuses" the muscles by varying the workouts so drastically that the muscles cannot adapt; that causes them to grow. Sound familiar? Yeah, pretty much the same thing I discussed about stepping out of your comfort zone. If you do the same routine every day, be it in your professional life or in the gym, eventually your muscles don't grow; instead, they adjust. Mark also does not place all his emphasis on weight lifting. At times we may go thirty days training like an "athlete," followed by forty-five days of "bodybuilding" and then thirty to forty-five days of a combination of both. Again, the muscles can't adjust to the constant change and as a result, my body continues to grow. I now know that to get maximum results and muscle tone from your workouts, no matter what type of exercise regimen you have, you should vary the stimuli.

I have come to associate muscle confusion with stepping out of your comfort zone to get beyond a business or personal plateau. While one helps you get fit and burn fat, the other advances you towards your clearly identified goals and definition of success.

Of course, what works for me is not necessarily going to work for everyone. When you take the time to identify your personal fitness goals, you may amaze yourself with what you are willing and able to do. I have found that having a personal trainer to motivate and challenge my limits has pushed me harder in directions I could not have imagined.

Taking the time to decide what you want out of your physical fitness goals will help point you in the right direction. Think about what you enjoy doing that involves physical activity. Some people prefer walking, jogging, golf, tennis, biking, racquetball, swimming, aerobics or some other type of exercise. As with anything relating to goals, the choice is personal. Whatever you choose to do, do it consistently and with intensity.

When people say they don't have time to exercise, I believe they simply do not want to exit their long-running comfort level. We all have the same amount of time; we just use it differently. What's incredible is when the same people who said they don't have time to exercise *do* find the time to watch every episode of their favorite TV show.

Thirty to forty intense minutes a day is all it takes: Get in. Exercise. Get out. Leave the cell phone in the car and forget socializing for a few minutes. When you're at the gym or health club (or jogging around your block), push yourself; sweat. In my opinion, at least 80 percent of a physical workout is mental. How you approach the workout, how you think about exercise and what it means to you is majority of the battle.

The Rewards of Discipline

If physical conditioning were easy, everybody would be doing it. Working out requires discipline and hard work. But the rewards are more than worth the effort. In addition to feeling better, you'll gain tremendous satisfaction from stretching yourself beyond past boundaries and reaching for new and higher levels. That's the breeding ground for confidence and momentum.

I don't just put in my time at the gym. I never go through the motions. Rather, I set workout goals, and I'm consistently striving to meet them then set new ones. When I do, my confidence increases, and I become more willing and able to venture outside of my comfort zone to tackle challenging goals in all areas of my life. No doubt about it, successful accomplishments outside of work fuel successful accomplishments at work.

You may wonder, if you are so motivated, Tony, why do you have a trainer? To which I would respond, even highly motivated people have trouble pushing beyond their comfort zones. That's why a personal trainer can be so helpful. Trainers show you the proper way to exercise in order to meet your physical goals. They challenge you to dig down deep and muster up energy and strength you didn't know you had.

Good trainers are encouraging but not pampering. Mark carefully watches my form on exercises. If it's wrong, he will correct it and make me do the work again. He gives me 100 percent of his attention. He isn't looking at the clock or checking his cell phone during our sessions.

Sometimes I dread it when he tells me to "work my weakest areas." Like most people, I'd rather stick with what I know are my strong points. But a good trainer will make you tackle areas where you need to improve. No one likes that. I certainly don't; but later, when I see the results, I understand and appreciate what he is doing.

When Mark and I started working with mitts, I found it a real struggle. I recall my first session being absolute hell. I was ready to quit (which should illustrate just how bad it was, because quitting isn't an option for me in any situation). After our session, in between gasps for air, I looked at Mark and said to him, "Don't ever do that to me again." Mark looked me over and gauged my physical condition. Here I was, panting and wheezing, feeling like I was going to die. I had never had that kind of a cardio workout and I was shocked at my level of exhaustion.

Just in case he didn't hear me, I repeated, "Seriously, don't ever do that to me again." Mark took a moment and responded, "We are *never* going to do three-minute rounds again." I was not sure what he meant, but for that moment in time, I was relieved.

Mark's response was not condescending or dictatorial; if anything, he was clear on taking the right steps to reach my goal. His clarity in finding out where I stood created a baseline for him to gauge my physical fitness and the direction we would go. Thinking back on Mark's statement that day (the one about "We are *never* going to do three-minute rounds again"), he kept his word—we have *never* done three-minute rounds again. Instead of three minutes, we now do rounds that are five minutes in duration and, thank goodness, my lungs have learned to remain in place.

Everyone can benefit from personal coaching, in business as well as in physical conditioning. Trainers are not essential, but they are definitely helpful. I see my trainer as an investment in my well-being. He pushes me beyond my limits, to a place I may not be able to reach on my own. It is my belief that no matter what regimen you choose, whether or not you use a trainer, it is imperative to incorporate a physical fitness program into your life. It will have a positive effect on your body and your mind. With a positive effect on your mind, you can't help but have a positive effect in your work and other areas of your life.

By tailoring your exercise program to match your specific goals and your personality, you can clearly communicate to a trainer or coach your desired intentions. You don't have to be as intense as I am about working out, just do something every day. Try it for three months and you'll be hooked. If you find you are ready for a trainer to push you the extra mile, then get one and use him or her to help you succeed.

CHAPTER 8: ENJOYING THE JOURNEY

When I am recruiting new consultants for my business, the first thing I tell them is, "This is a great business. The hours are flexible, the compensation is good, you'll work with the greatest people on the planet, and most importantly, you will have fun." All the things I've discussed so far—goals, focus, energy, action—need to be taken seriously. In my mind, when discussing success, the journey is just as important as the destination. You've got to be able to laugh and have fun along the way. No matter how much money I'm earning, if I'm not having fun and enjoying the process, I will go and do something else. My life is about fulfillment and being happy.

I wish I had a dime for every time someone preached to me, "You should stop and smell the roses." Those people obviously don't know me very well. They're looking in from the outside and assuming that because I'm highly focused and working hard, I'm not having fun. They may think that I need to function and have fun in the manner that they do. But the thing is, I enjoy what I do and so I *am* smelling the roses all along the way. It doesn't take a weekend or a holiday for me to stop and smell the roses. It's Tuesday, I just reached a benchmark—guess what, I just smelled a rose. It's Wednesday, I just had a great workout—I just got a bunch of roses. It's Saturday, I just had drinks with friends, I might as well become a florist with this bunch of flowers. See my point? Stopping and enjoying your life doesn't require a special day or time. If you are having fun and enjoying whatever you are doing, then you are in the rose garden 100 percent. My profession is not work to me. It's not a job; it's a career. It's part of my lifestyle.

The fact that I can work with people who have a sense of humor and are fun to be around makes the journey more enjoyable. I don't have to *stop* to smell the roses. I smell a rose at every step along the way.

Another thing that makes me want to pull my hair out (if I had any hair) is when people say, "No one on their deathbed ever wished he'd spent more time at the office." I'm convinced that most of those people who say things like that look at their work as a chore, or maybe this is what gives them balance when they get too intense in their work. They may use that line to rationalize why they need to slow down. They're possibly the same people who clock watch and can't wait to get home at night so they can sit on the couch and watch television. In short, they don't love what they do, and they may use that statement to regulate themselves when they get too engrossed into something. It's understandable.

Wayne Muller wrote, "Life is what's happening when you're too busy to notice." But that doesn't describe my life. I'm never too busy to notice. In fact, I'm not only noticing, I'm enjoying the hell out of life.

Although I work my butt off, I also recharge my battery often. I strive to never feel pulled in several directions, and I don't suffer from lack of motivation, shortage of energy, reduced efficiency or an increase in mistakes. Those are all signs of overwork and insufficient rest.

Given the intensity of my workday and my nightly workouts, I would keel over if I didn't take a step back and rest. Balance is the key to everything. If I reach a point where I am tired or feel like I may not be able to focus, I take a "guilt-free" break. One of my favorite recharge methods is to take a trip down to the Keys with some friends and cut loose. A few drinks at Captain Tony's (good name for a bar, huh?) and some sun and sea are the surefire elixir for me.

While some people find their "juice" in hunting, fishing or something else, I find mine primarily in building my career. And I'm fortunate to be surrounded by good people who make doing so a terrific experience for me on a daily basis.

I truly believe in the expression, "You get what you focus on." I choose to focus on making my career (and my life) fun. I don't divide my life into "work" and "fun." I don't look forward to having fun only after I leave the office, or after I retire. As serious as I am about business, I try to see the light-hearted side of things. When I'm on the road, traveling the country and consulting with clients, practical joking and humor can turn a routine grind into a memorable experience.

One Doll Too Many

A few years ago, one of my clients sent me to a remote part of Georgia to straighten out a series of operational Medicare issues. Melanie, a manager for the region in question, was asked to travel with me in order to assist in rectifying the operational concerns. Melanie is a wonderful woman—she really is very nice—but she is afraid of anything that moves. No kidding, you could look at Melanie and go, "Boo," and she'd jump.

As we traveled together for a couple of weeks, we got to know each other and we kidded a lot on our work excursions. One of our stops was at a home health agency in Georgia. While Melanie was talking to the employees, I took a look around the place. In one of the rooms, sitting on the floor leaning against the wall, was a Resuscitation Annie doll, one of those mannequins medical schools used as a teaching aid in CPR classes.

Even to me, the thing was eerie. It was so lifelike it was startling. At first, I thought a real person was sitting there on the floor. As a kid, I remember seeing one of those dolls in health class. The teacher wanted us to give it mouth-to-mouth, and while as a youngster I was repulsed, now I was just plain spooked.

I asked one of the women who worked for the agency if I could borrow Annie for the night. Melanie was this woman's boss and here she was lending out Annie. Being a good sport, she said OK to my request. What's more, once she heard of my plan, she helped to distract Melanie while I took care of putting Annie in the trunk of the rental car.

At lunchtime, I took Annie back to the hotel. There, with Annie tucked under my arm, I asked the front desk to let me into Melanie's room. I really can't imagine what this man might have thought at this request with the slightly scary looking doll's dead eyes peering at him from under the counter, but he was cool and composed as he informed me, "We can't do that." I argued that it was important; I mean, I was carrying a CPR doll—doesn't that look like official business? I pleaded my case about how Melanie and I were traveling together and I was in charge of putting Annie away. He finally conceded with, "Well, OK, we'll let you in as long as we can have a maintenance man go with you." Annie now had a bodyguard.

So the maintenance man-turned-bodyguard, Annie and I proceeded to Melanie's room. While my security companion waited, I sat Annie on the toilet, tied her up straight with a long catheter tube that was coming out of her, and placed a newspaper in her hand. When I was finished, the doll appeared to be sitting on the toilet reading the newspaper.

After lunch, Melanie and I went back to the home health agency. We both got involved in our work, and I forgot all about Annie. At the end of the day, I dropped Melanie off at the hotel and went off to do my gym routine. I told Melanie that I would phone her when I returned and we could then go have dinner.

When I came back from the gym, the light was blinking on the phone in my room. It was a message from Melanie. "You'd better get your ass over here right now!"

When I got to Melanie's floor I found her standing out in the hall, shaking her head. "You almost gave me a heart attack! When I went into the bathroom, I thought that mannequin was a real person sitting on the toilet! That thing is creepy! I can't believe you did that!" She refused to even go back inside her room until I removed Annie.

Melanie was traumatized for about a day and a half, but eventually she too got a good laugh. But that incident, mingled with work, made the trip fun. People in that company still talk about Annie and Melanie. **It's just part of the journey.**

To Err is Humor

Most people don't want others to know when they mess up. They try to cover up their mistakes. But I don't mind if others see my imperfections. Actually, I have fun sharing stories about the ridiculous things I've done. They make for great happy hour conversation.

In my view, this attitude comes from a healthy sense of self. So many people take themselves too seriously, perhaps because they're trying to protect their self-image. I am not suggesting that you should behave like a clown, but let's face it—we all do things that are embarrassing and funny. If you want to enjoy life, you've got to have the courage to laugh at yourself. Humor is essential.

If I were to be totally serious with all of my colleagues and all of my clients, our relationships wouldn't be nearly as good. Because we have good rapport, we laugh and enjoy our collaboration on projects, and that makes them enjoyable experiences. Humor doesn't impede our work; it facilitates it. It creates an outlet and a balance.

Even challenges can be fun. Hitting the mitts in the gym is absolutely grueling work, but it's also fun and beneficial. Things don't have to be easy to be fun. **Strive to see the positive and lighthearted side of things.**

If the job or the project I'm working on isn't fun, I look for a way to make it so. When I'm presented with a challenge, I ask myself, "How can I overcome this challenge *and* have fun in the process?" When I phrase the question that way, my mind starts looking for ways to make it happen.

A few years ago, I had a client who was less than enjoyable to work with and managed to raise a number of challenges. His difficult disposition and combative nature presented me with an opportunity to further develop my skills in handling such a personality. He seemed to enjoy dominating people and letting them know that he was in charge. He felt that he needed to do this in order to be seen as a leader.

I have learned that leadership and dominance are totally different things. Leadership creates momentum; dominance only creates motion. In order to keep my sanity, I made up my mind not to focus on how infuriating he was. I knew it would be counterproductive to dwell in the negative. Instead, I asked myself, "How can I deal with this guy *and* enjoy the process?" Answering that question changed my mindset. It cleared my space of negative "stuff." Instead of dwelling on the problem, I began working on a solution. Instead of being controlled by my emotions, I took control of them.

Although our relationship didn't completely turn around, it became much more manageable. I became the co-leader rather than the victim. No matter how nasty he got, I didn't reciprocate.

It appears to me that a lot of people live "accidentally." They take what life gives them and say, "This sucks, but there's nothing I can do." They'd rather complain about things than change them. I refer to these people as "victims of fate."

You can either choose to take responsibility and focus on the solution, or you can be a victim and focus on the problem. You can decide to control your emotions, or you can let your emotions control you.

Listen, you have every right in the world to experience frustration, hurt, anger and any other negative emotion. You wouldn't be human if you didn't. I'm just saying that, for your own sake, once you experience it get past it and move on.

Controlling emotions requires mental discipline and emotional energy. That's one reason I'm such an advocate for physical conditioning. When you're in good physical shape, you have more energy to meet challenges and make positive choices. Working out just a few days a week makes me feel better, and when I feel better, I act and react better. Body, mind and emotions work together synergistically.

Enjoying the Journey

When I first started my company, I didn't have any "pie in the sky" vision for the future. I just knew that I was tired of corporate politics and that I wanted to be my own boss. If I had a goal, it was probably nothing loftier than to earn enough money to buy a boat. I figured that if my business went to hell, I could at least cruise on my boat.

Twelve years after starting Professional Provider Services, I still don't own a boat. Actually, I don't even want one, because something interesting happened along the way that changed my perspective. I started having so much fun building the business that other things became less important. Because my priorities had changed, and I now pursued the satisfaction of achievement, things like owning a boat and just making money (while still nice) were no longer at the top of my priority list. The journey became more important than the destination.

Over the years, as my business has grown, I've grown with it. In the midst of the satisfying process of building something of value, I received many wonderful intangibles. These have varied and include valuable relationships, knowledge from others, and the experience of building a business. And one of the most valuable lessons I've learned is that your business should serve your life, not *run* your life.

I certainly do not claim to have all the answers. I'm still learning and growing. But I hope that my experiences and observations will encourage you, and that they will help you make your journey more successful. Most importantly, you should have fun—lots of it—along the way.

CHAPTER 9: FOREVER IN BLUE JEANS

It feels like it was yesterday that I graduated college and embarked on my short-lived accounting career. I recall massaging my limited budget to get it to accommodate my grocery list—macaroni and cheese, Ramen noodles—and conservative visits to the local bar. In amazement, I smile at the updated inventory that comprises my life and has now led to this book. It just seems so wild.

One afternoon, at a small family gathering, someone asked me, "What would you do if you won the lottery?" Without much hesitation and continuing to look down at my lap I replied, "I could use a couple more pairs of jeans." My response urged the person to prod further in an effort to find the "real" answer. To their disappointment, I couldn't come up with an answer that was more exciting. The jeans were really all I needed, and fortunately, I didn't need the lottery to get them.

The experience of building my business has brought about a number of hard-earned benefits. Most people would recognize financial freedom as the biggest asset resulting from the invested hard work. However, this freedom has not changed the person that I am. I remain grounded and free-spirited, enjoying my journey (at times losing my head) but always returning to square one—humility.

In the Fall of 2005, I was in the market for a condominium in an upscale building in Fort Lauderdale. I met my real estate agent to view one of the available units, and while riding up in the elevator we engaged in the customary client-agent banter. The agent began citing the names of the celebrities who lived in the building, which ranged from a former athlete to a current pop icon. But glamour has never been something that impresses me, and my expression never changed as she ticked off the list of names.

The tour only pointed up to me what I already knew: that in the end, I was content with my comfortable home, my quiet street and my simple lifestyle. If anything, I walked away with a clearer idea of what was important to me: my peace of mind and comfort, not the place I called home.

Don't get me wrong—I did indulge in a phase of good old American consumerism. I purchased different cars, stayed in high-end hotels and experienced those things that I had always dreamed of, and I had a hell of a good time in the process. However, once the experiences were out of my system, I again moved forward.

What I came to realize about reaching a different financial goal is how much of it was related to the ego. I felt a sense of power to walking into a car dealership and paying cash for a sports car. The next time you visit the same dealership, ten salesmen will do everything short of rolling out a red carpet for you.

At first, it's a rush. But at some point I realized that having people fawn over me gets old. You can't take it as a compliment, because after all, what they're really interested in is your checkbook. And who can blame them for that? No, the big reward isn't the ego boost. It's the freedom of being able to know that you can do what you like when you want to do it, because you earned that privilege. Knowing you can buy something you need without worry. Knowing that others respect your talents and abilities because you've proved yourself so many times that you don't need to prove anything to anyone anymore—except, perhaps, to yourself. I learned the importance of knowing what was valuable to me.

And what is valuable to me often does not have a price tag. One day about four years ago, while on a layover in the Atlanta airport, I watched two little twin girls playing at my boarding gate. Still reeling from having just signed a lucrative business contract in Baltimore, I watched as the girls carried on with carefree laughter. Their smiles and joy reminded me of my own daughter, and I continued to observe them in silent appreciation. I noticed that one of the girls had lost her hair. She had clearly been sick. The child drew close upon realizing I was observing. Happily, she grinned and offered me one of her toys. I smiled back at her and wondered what she must be going through, what her life was like, and how difficult it had to be for her parents to address her situation. I fought back tears as she started to play with me.

"Don't bother him, Hailey," her mother told her.

"She isn't bothering me at all," I quickly assured her.

That experience is as clear to me now as if it had happened yesterday, for its poignancy and also because it pointed up the contrast between business matters and human matters. Taking a moment to observe and reflect on those around me has given me a chance to obtain a fresh perspective and understand what in life has true value. Money isn't everything. When we don't have it, we work hard to get it. Once we get it, we often find we have more friends than we know what to do with—or we don't know what to do with it right away. In the end, knowing who you are and what is of genuine importance to you will prevail. You most likely will find that it is not the same thing you originally thought it was.

Within Ten Minutes

In the world of business, there are certain benchmarks by which levels of success are measured. A watch, the car a person drives, the neighborhood they live in, the school to which they send their children—society often looks to these as measures of a person's professional success.

A close friend once remarked to me that a good businessman doesn't have to wear a watch to tell the time. His awareness of the day and his surroundings would have him knowing the time within ten minutes of any given hour. I take pride in the fact that I have yet to fall outside of those ten minutes. That simple ability helps me to better define my idea of being a good businessman. I work hard to avoid gauging my advancements by the make of the car I am able to afford or the designer labels I could wear. This is my personal view and experience; it is not intended to judge or diminish what another person may use to measure personal accomplishment. Success is not only relative; it is personal.

People see what people see; they do not see what I feel. This is true for all of us. I remember in the summer of 2008 realizing that my favorite pair of blue jeans was torn beyond acceptable wearing conditions. To say I was disappointed would be an understatement.

One day, as I stood at the reception desk in my office, I encountered the delivery person for a dry cleaning service. I told him I had a pair of jeans that needed mending in a few key areas. He assured that this could easily be done and that he would pick up my jeans the next day.

The following day, I went to the office and placed my jeans at the counter for the receptionist to provide at the scheduled pickup. She held them up, glancing from the pants to me and back again. "Are you kidding?" she asked, incredulous. "It's going to cost more to fix these than to buy a new pair."

"No," I said. "These are my favorite jeans. I really want them fixed."

It never dawned on me that the rips were so extensive that my request would seem unreasonable. They were my favorite jeans, and I had to try to get them repaired. I left the receptionist chuckling behind me and shaking her head in amusement. She was laughing to herself at me, but she was the one who didn't get it. She didn't understand the joy and comfort that the well-worn jeans brought me. It was a textbook case of someone who could only see the obvious and not being able to feel what someone else feels. The satisfaction of knowing those torn jeans would be repaired was my own and only to be understood by me. Just like success. It's a personal feeling, an intimate reward.

I could not ever reach my goals if I were to measure success by someone else's yardstick; what should be done and what it will look like when I get there. If I did, I would be following someone else's standards and not my own. Would I ever reach the pinnacle of success by walking another person's path? No. I have always maintained a clear image and understanding of who I am and what I want, and I use that image to guide me every day.

By being aware of the hour and the life around me, I have learned to:

- Stay focused. By not losing sight of what makes me happy, I derive joy from the challenge of every day, the opportunity to obtain a new client, to solve a different problem, to help someone move ahead with peace of mind and balance.

- Be aware. I am always aware of what's around me. I do not become complacent with my surroundings, my life and my activities. I find the richness in every experience. Whether at the gym or at the office, I take note of what is happening and thus feel more involved and alive with what I am to do and where.

- Remain grateful. I understand that every experience is an opportunity for a higher step, and so I view the situation and challenge as growth versus a reason to complain or lose sight of my goal due to unimportant occurrences.

These intangibles are like my blue jeans: often torn, definitely comfortable and always the things I want clear in my mind and by my side. After all, they have helped me define success in a manner that cannot be purchased at a store.

On the Horizon

All this being said, I am the first one to tell you that I am far from being done with the development of my life, business and body. On the business horizon, Professional Provider Services continues to grow and associate with more talented members and offering differing perspectives. The standards for my physical fitness continue to rise as I meet and exceed the standards of yesterday, and my life takes new exciting routes and experiences.

And when it's all said and done, without question, I'll be found where this delightful journey into creating my life began, somewhere tropical, with a drink in hand, and laughing wholeheartedly over someone probably asking, "So, what band were you with?"